THE

{ **CHEAP** }
{ **Bastard's** }

GUIDE™ TO THE

GOOD HOUSE ✚ HOME

{ CONTENTS }

CHAPTER 5: A Tidy Sum

CHAPTER 6: Growth Funds

CHAPTER 7: The Fix Is In

CHAPTER 8: Getting an Upgrade

{ FOREWORD: Cheap Bastard in the House }

> 'Mid pleasures and palaces though we
> may roam. Be it ever so humble, there's
> no place like home.
>
> —*T. H. Payne*

Having spent my whole life mastering the art of Cheap Bastardry, I was thrilled with the idea of extending the concept of my book *The Cheap Bastard's Guide™ to New York City,* to a home book. Besides the fact that I would be able to weasel myself a free copy, I knew that nothing sucks more cash out of your pocket than your home. In whatever shape it takes and whatever stage of life you are in, your home can easily turn into that hole in the ground you pour your money into. No subject screams out louder for Cheap Bastard solutions, and Josh Garskof has done a terrific job coming up with ingenious ways to save tons of money on just about every square foot of your home.

For me, the perfect Cheap Bastard home has evolved with every phase of my life, from a prized dirt-cheap fifth-floor walk-up micro-studio apartment just out of college to thoughts of a house in the 'burbs as my wife and I start to plan for a family. Cheap means different things to us at different points in our lives, and this book will help you out wherever you fall on the Cheap Bastard evolutionary timeline.

When I set out to get my first it's-time-to-move-out-of-my-parents'-house-but-I-can't-really-afford-anything place, my motto was basic and simple—"Don't make me pay for anything." As a result, I rented the cheapest, smallest, most out-of-the-way and inconvenient apartment I could get my hands on. Needless to say, hiring an interior decorator was not in my nonexistent budget; I really could've used a few tips from the decorating chapter then. Left to my own devices, I settled on a style I call Early Hand-Me-Down with a ragtag selection of furnishings, dishes, and linens from my parents, brothers, and charitable friends. It wasn't pretty, but it was all mine.

Over time, I have lived in apartments that have sometimes been more convenient, some more spacious, but always progressively more expensive. As a result I mastered one particular technique to help me deck out my new digs—while barely having to crack open my wallet. I became a street-finds specialist, a castaway connoisseur, a dumpster-diving demon. Through trial and painful error (Tip: Don't try lugging a large desk up five flights of stairs without first measuring to see if it will fit through the front door—Ouch!) and the addition of a few select pieces from local thrift stores and flea markets, I managed to put together a pretty eclectic and oddly stylish look. The bonus? Everything I owned had a story; each a true conversation piece.

Then came the most challenging phase of my ever evolving Cheap Bastard life: that's right, love came to The Cheap Bastard. My wife, Karen, is definitely not a Cheap Bastard, so we had to figure out ways to not only combine our stuff, but also our sensibilities. Now we are even starting to think about the next move. Could it be? The Cheap Bastard in suburbia, owning a real house, with an overgrown yard, a rickety swing on the front porch, and a kitchen in need of renovations. All I can say is, I (and my bank account) am glad I'll have *The Cheap Bastard's Guide™ to the Good House and Home* to see me through it all.

Rob Grader
New York City
www.thecheapbastard.com

{ **INTRODUCTION:** }
The Land of the Free

Right now I have enough money to last me the
rest of my life—unless I buy something.

—*Jackie Mason*

There's nothing like buying a home to make you feel broke. Just
when you've cleared out your savings and taken on a host of big new monthly bills,
you get hit with the unbudgeted expenses that manage to sneak up on every new
homeowner: the lawn mower, the gallons of paint, the bedroom window coverings,
the air conditioners, the tree guy . . .

Meanwhile, you probably can't turn around inside your new house (or condo or
co-op) without seeing something you'd like to upgrade or redecorate—especially if
you partake in any of the glossy books and magazines dedicated to flaunting the
latest products you can't afford. Well, the Cheap Bastard is here to tell you that it's
not worth living on ramen noodles for the next twenty years in order to pay off
that two-person massaging bathtub with built-in wine chiller, wide-screen television, and surround sound. (And the truth is, nobody ever uses those trophy tubs
anyway.) Nor should you be misled by the countless television shows purporting
to teach affordable decorating techniques. The made-for-TV simplicity of those programs can lead to some pretty questionable procedures, such as installing crown
molding without nailing it directly into the wood framing or constructing furniture
out of plywood and staples. The results may look okay on camera, but they'll
quickly fall apart in the real world.

The Cheap Bastard's Guide to the Good House and Home won't tease you with
unattainable merchandise, nor will it suggest shoddy practices in the name of
saving money. Instead, this book will teach you economical ways to buy, furnish,
beautify, organize, repair, and improve your home, using quality products and
sound techniques. It's not about how to be a freeloader or a miser; it's about
being flexible and trying some creative methods for stretching your scratch. You

can't always get everything that you want, but we're going to show you how to save money on what you need—and how to fund a few out-and-out splurges, too.

The cheapest things in life are the free ones, of course, and you'll find out how to get free phone service, free Internet access, interest-free loans, free mulch, free building materials, free tax help, and a whole lot more. We've also got tips for getting amazing deals on things you actually do need to pay for. But the biggest returns by far will come from the hundreds of household cost-cutting tricks we're going to show you, from making your own cleaning supplies using standard pantry ingredients to bartering for your plumber's services instead of paying cash; from expanding your home without building an addition to turning homeownership into a tax windfall. Sometimes, alas, there is a catch to the deal, and we'll warn you about these pitfalls, too.

Even with all of the focus on the bottom line, though, this book is not about how to live a Spartan lifestyle. It's about creating an attractive and warm home that you can actually afford. It's about the thrill of the hunt—and about having some interesting stories to tell. When a guest compliments your new club chair, for example, you'll be able to explain how you found it on the curb on bulk trash day, carted it home balanced on a hastily borrowed wheelbarrow, then reupholstered it with a fabric remnant you picked up gratis on Freecyle.org. When your new flowering pear tree gets noticed, you can talk about how you rooted it from a twig that you cut yourself, perhaps in the front yard of the home where your great-grandparents once lived. And regarding your unusual collection of, say, antique cobalt-blue glass bottles or tourist snow globes, you can boast that you got them supercheap by being a savvy eBayer and flea marketer.

In short, this is a guide to homeownership for real people with real budgets. It's about how to lead a frugal lifestyle—and it's about crucial elements of homeownership that are so often overlooked, like how to share expenses among housemates (with one set of guidelines for people who share beds and another set for those who don't), how taking some simple steps now will prevent the need for expensive home repairs later, and how to win your battles with nasty customer service agents when you've been mistreated by your credit card or cable company.

You'll learn how to save *thousands of dollars* while creating a one-of-a-kind home that you never thought you could afford. Best of all, the results will truly be your own and will make you far more house-proud than you'd ever be if you had selected some cookie-cutter furnishings from those glossy books and magazines. Instead, use those publications as decorating elements themselves, by setting them out on the coffee table for visitors to browse? Then, when you're tired of them, you can cut them up for decoupage art projects, put them through the shredder to make packing materials, or donate them to a library or nursing home as a tax write-off!

{ MOVERS AND SHAKERS: }
BUYING UP, SELLING OUT, AND MOVING IN

The universe is merely a fleeting idea
in God's mind—a pretty uncomfortable
thought, particularly if you've just
made a down payment on a house.

—*Woody Allen*

It's the most money you've ever spent, more money than you can believe you've promised to pay over the next thirty years, and you don't know how you'll ever afford curtains for the living room or a repairman for a whatever problem might arise. So it's definitely time to start pinching your pennies. From buying this home to selling the last one (if this isn't your first) to making the move, here's how to save as much money as possible before you spend even your first night in your new home. That way, you'll be able to afford window treatments or a twenty-four-hour emergency plumbing service when the time comes.

A HOME IN THE (PRICE) RANGE

Let's start at the beginning, finding a home you can afford—and love. If you're still in the house-buying stage, here's how to keep both the price and the mortgage rate as low as possible.

How Far Can You Throw Your Agent?

Homebuyers: you need to understand that your real estate agent doesn't really work for you. Oh, sure, she e-mails you whenever houses in your price range come on the market, and she takes you to tour places that you might want to buy, and she does your negotiating for you. Still, she doesn't necessarily have your best interests in mind—because her own interests often conflict with yours.

Your agent will get paid when you buy a house. And so she wants you to find a place and buy it. The sooner you do that, the sooner she gets paid and the less work she will have to do in taking you to see more houses. And since she wants the deal to happen, there's little incentive for her to point out potential problems with the home—advising you to hire an inspector to investigate a potential flaw with the septic system, for example, or warning you about that shooting range a quarter mile up the road. And why should she tell you the lowest possible price she thinks you could pay for the house when the more you pay, the larger her commission will be? This is not to say that all agents are duplicitous or unreliable. But you need to understand which side your agent's bread is buttered on so you don't make the mistake of putting too much trust in what she says.

A new breed of agent purports to eliminate these conflicts of interest. Called buyer's agents, they often take special courses and sign a code of ethics about representing the interests of buyers. Exclusive buyer's agents (you can find one at www.naeba.org) take things a step farther: Neither these agents nor their firms represent any sellers, which eliminates the temptation to steer clients to houses listed by their own firms.

THE CATCH In most cases buyer's agents get paid a commission on your sale, so their interests really aren't any different from other agents. }

(OR RIDICULOUSLY CHEAP)

■ **GET IT FOR FREE**

A FANTASTIC HOUSE

Selling a vacant house is harder than selling one that's lived in—and on average means a 10 to 15 percent lower sale price—so some real estate agents who are listing high-end properties have begun bringing in "home managers" to give vacant houses that lived-in look. Sign up to be a home manager, and you might just get yourself free or nearly free rent to live in an amazing house. Of course, you'll need to be ready to move whenever the house sells and to keep things neat and clean for showings that can occur at any time. Go to www.showhomes.com, check www.craigslist.org, or call local real estate agencies and ask if they hire home managers.

THE CATCH You can't be a smoker or have pets—and you may need to provide the furniture. }

Shopping for Home Loans

Whether you're looking for a new home mortgage, to refinance your existing mortgage, or to take out a home equity loan, you can save thousands of dollars by shopping around for the best possible price. Web sites like Bankrate.com and eLoan.com are good for getting a sense of the current rates, but don't take your loan from an online lender. You can get a better rate—as well as better customer service and a smaller risk of having a problem at closing—from a local bank.

Skip the mortgage brokers—they are simply middlemen who resell bank loans and add their own fees onto the transaction. Just open up the local phone book and call every bank in your area to find out what their rates are. Make sure you don't skip the small savings banks, because they're likely to have the best rates. (They have to in order to compete with the large brand-name banks with big advertising muscle.) And for mortgages, don't ask only about the interest rate, but also for a complete list of the bank's closing costs. Look for either a thirty-year fixed loan rate or an adjustable rate with an introductory fixed rate that's longer than you anticipate being in the house—say, five, seven, or ten years for a starter home.

Should You Pay Points?

Are you better off paying "points" to the bank to lower your mortgage rate or just adding the cash to your down payment?

As long as you're going to stay put for a few years—without refinancing—those points will pay for themselves down the road. Just make sure you have enough cash to also cover your down payment and to keep an emergency fund of a few thousand dollars as well as the points. To run the numbers for your purchase and see how long it'll take for those points to pay you back, use the "Mortgage Points Adviser" worksheet at www.bankrate.com (click on "Calculators").

What about Interest-Only Loans?

These mortgages come with extremely low interest rates, so they can seem like bargains, but they're actually fraught with financial peril.

There are two reasons that these loans can boast such low monthly payments.

First, they're actually teaser interest rates that may last only three to five years; then they shoot up to the prevailing rates as adjustable-rate mortgages. Second, for that same introductory period, your monthly payment doesn't include any contribution toward the principal that you owe. But when the introductory period is over, your monthly payment is going to skyrocket. That's because principal is now added to the bill, and also because the interest rate will be higher, quite possibly much higher.

The mortgage companies that sell these loans are quick to point out that you can always refinance the loan—that is, trade it for a new mortgage with better terms—before the introductory period ends, but that's an expensive undertaking in its own right. And if interest rates have soared in the meantime, you may not be able to find a traditional loan that you can afford at that time. Plus, you're not paying down any principal during the introductory period—so if the real estate market slumps after you buy, you could wind up owing more on your mortgage than you can get for your house. That might mean you cannot refinance—or sell—when you want to.

SELLING HIGH

When you're a first-time homebuyer, finding and purchasing a house feels like the biggest financial stress you can ever experience. Then, someday, you trade up to a bigger home, and in addition to buying a new place, you have to sell the old one—a complex two-phased transaction that's about five times as nerve-wracking as buying alone.

Save $10,000 by Skipping the Agent

How's this for a high-paying job? Give anywhere from a handful to a few dozen tours of your home, staff one or two open houses so people can drop in to see it without an appointment, and pocket a cool $10,000. Well, you can earn that kind of ching when it's time to sell your house, co-op, or condo simply by serving as your own agent. The agents for the buyers and sellers typically split 5 percent of the total sale price of a home, out of the seller's pocket, bringing the total commission on a $200,000 home to $10,000, so if you skip the agent, it's like putting that money right into your own pocket. (The commission is negotiable, by the way, and usually falls between 4 and 6 percent.)

The downsides are:

- You don't have a real estate agent to walk you through the sales process, from helping to determine your asking price to helping potential buyers see all of the home's potential.

- Since the buyer's agent earns money by sharing the commission the seller pays, going without an agent means that no buyer's real estate agents are going to bring their clients to see your home. You'll have to attract your own customers.

- Since many buyers have signed contracts saying that they will only buy a house through their agent, you've seriously limited your potential pool of buyers by working outside the system.

- You'll have to take care of the advertising yourself, which means placing ads in the local newspaper and paying to list the home on Web sites designed for sell-it-yourselfers.

On the other hand:

- Those ads will cost only hundreds, not thousands of dollars.

- The biggest stresses and hassles of selling a home are no different with or without a real estate agent: You need to have the house and yard spotless and presentable at all times; you need to be prepared for people to come through to see it on a moment's notice; and you need to decide what to do when the inevitable lowball offers come in.

So why not try the sell-it-yourself route? Start by interviewing a few local real estate agents for the possible exclusive right to sell your house. You can tell them that you're weighing the possibility of selling yourself but haven't decided. Throughout the interview process, agents will provide you with lists of recent sales of comparable houses in your area and give you their opinions on the fair price of your home and how to best present it for sale. You can then use this information to put the house on the market yourself. If you find an agent you really like, you can always work with him in the event that selling it yourself doesn't work out.

In the meantime, here are some resources that can help you sell it yourself:

Zillow.com

Plug your address into this free Web site, and it'll access public information about your home, as well as the prices of homes that have sold recently in your area—and what features they have. All of these data instantly get crunched together to produce what the site deems a fair price for your home.

AppraisalInstitute.org

For a few hundred dollars, you can get a professional assessment based on recent sales of comparable homes. This Web site will link you to appraisers in your area who are members of the Appraisal Institute, a trade group.

ForSaleByOwner.com

The largest real estate listing site around (after the agents' site www.realtor.com), this is the first place for to go whether you want to place an ad to sell your own home or you're a buyer and wonder what owner-offered properties your agent isn't showing you.

Audrie.com

For about $60, you get a sell-it-yourself kit containing directions about everything from getting your house presentable to pricing it right, essential sales forms and contracts that are appropriate for your state, a Web advertisement listing your home, and even a for sale sign for your front lawn.

Foxtons.com and ZipRealty.com

These services are something like a cross between sell-it-yourself sites such as For Sale By Owner and full-scale real estate agents. You list your house on their site to attract buyers who aren't contractually bound to full-priced real estate agents—and you also get some broker services, such as newspaper ads, open houses, and by-appointment tours. These agencies charge as little as half the price of standard agencies.

WHAT YOUR AGENT WON'T TELL YOU ABOUT OPEN HOUSES

If you hire a real estate agent to sell your home, one of the first things she'll do is set up an open house, ostensibly so that potential buyers can come and see your place. But that's not the real purpose of open houses. The vast majority of people who attend these events are just dipping their toes into the home-shopping waters and aren't ready to make an offer on anything—or they're "window-shoppers," other sellers trying to get a sense of what they should charge for their home, or plain old nosy neighbors. Your agent's real goal for the open house is to meet those newbie home shoppers, get their names and phone numbers, and sign them on as clients.

Flipping Your House

Will all those big bucks you spent at the home center and those weekends you spent clinging to ladders translate into a profit when you sell your old house?

To be sure, many people have done well by buying fixer-uppers, putting in the money and sweat equity to transform them, and then flipping them. But that takes good vision for the potential of a home and a neighborhood—and it takes good luck. Plenty of people have lost their shirts this way, too.

Even a study by *Remodeling* magazine, a construction trade publication, and the National Association of Realtors—two groups with vested interests in promoting the idea of house flipping—shows that most homeowners don't get back the full cost of their home improvements when they sell a year later. For example, the 2005 study indicated that home sellers recouped only 94 percent of the cost of finishing an attic with a bedroom and bathroom and 83 percent of the cost of a family room addition. Bathroom remodels, however, did recoup the full investment and more. You can see the data on both project prices and returns by going to www.Realtor.org and entering "cost versus value" in the search field.

You can't exactly take these national numbers to the bank, though. For one thing, they aren't based on real data, just on Internet surveys of real estate agents and contractors. Plus, there's a good chance that the return on investment for these projects could increase over time since real estate tends to appreciate in value. Construction costs also vary dramatically from one zip code to the next, and different house features have wildly different values depending on the neighborhood. For example, a new high-end bathroom will yield a much bigger return in areas where ceramic tiles and jet tubs are the norm than they will in neighborhoods where most bathrooms haven't been updated.

You don't need to knock on neighbors' doors to find out the typical features of houses in your area. Just take a look at the town's property tax assessments. These will give you the municipality's take on house values and vital statistics, such as overall square footage, number of bathrooms, and whether they have pools, hot tubs, or finished basements. All of that information is public and available at town hall or, in many cases, is linked to the town's Web site.

The bottom line is that the best approach to big renovations is to think of them as investments in a better quality of life in your home—not a chance to turn a profit. Then enjoy the changes, and if they wind up being a good financial investment as well, consider it gravy.

Sprucing to Sell

Some quick and inexpensive updates can make your house more salable:

- Apply cosmetics. Simple jobs such as painting walls, changing cabinet pulls, replacing faucets and light fixtures, and changing outlet and switch cover plates can help you dress up the space.

- Add by subtracting. Pulling up dingy wall-to-wall carpeting, removing dated window cornices, and getting rid of makeshift items like window insulating plastic and shoddy wall shelving can have just as big an impact as the things you add.

- Focus on kitchens and baths. These are the rooms that sell houses, and they are the spaces where you should focus your attention.

- Stay neutral. Beiges, tans, whites, browns, and natural wood and stone are neutral colors, which means that they'll meld well with anyone's tastes—so they're good decorating colors for houses going on the market.

- Cover flaws. Got wall cracks in the hallway? Think about wallpapering the room. Crumbling plaster at the base of the bathroom walls? Install bead-board wainscoting. This is not dishonesty—hey, you can tell the buyers about the underlying problems if you want to—it's merely showing everything in the best possible light.

- De-clutter. One of the best things you can do to make your house look good is to clean it up. Clear out the junk in the basement and get your gear and tools stored neatly. Remove the piles of accumulated stuff around the house and thin out your furniture collection to make the floor plan feel roomier.

- Set the stage. Got a friend with some really great antiques or oil paintings? Borrowing them and placing them in your house when you show it can subtly impress buyers.

MOVIN' ON UP

The cheapest way to move, without a doubt, is to corral some able-bodied friends into helping out with the job. But not every move is suitable for amateurs, and finding professional movers who are both affordable and reliable can be a struggle. Here's how to save an arm, a leg—and a lower back—on your move.

7 Rules of Moving Etiquette

You know who your real friends are on moving day: They're the ones who show up to help you haul all your stuff to the new place. So don't take advantage of these guys. Stick to the unwritten rules of the road.

1. You can ask friends to help you move from one apartment to another; from any home you share with roommates or parents to any other place; or into your first real house. But when you move into your second house, it's time to hire professionals.

2. Avoid asking friends to help you move farther than 100 miles, unless one set of local friends helps you load the truck on one end and another set helps to unload it at your destination. And if you do ask a pal or two to hit the road with you, be sure to pick up the tab for all the hotels, meals, and jumbo coffees or Red Bulls along the way.

3. Get everything packed and ready to go before your friends arrive. You don't want them to wind up having to help wrap knickknacks in newspaper, load books into boxes, or remove pictures from the walls before the actual move can begin.

4. Keep a stash of bottled water handy to help everyone stay hydrated, serve a light lunch when you reach a good resting point, and throw down a feast

of quality pizza and quality beer (or other beverages) when the work is done.

5. Don't skimp on the size of the truck (unless you're only moving a few miles). Too small a vehicle means a lot more travel time back and forth for your crew.

6. Work as hard as or harder than everyone else (remember: lift with the legs, not the back), and also encourage everyone to take a break now and then—and stop with them.

7. Return the favor. Folks who help you move should get your help with their moves—or painting their house, or whatever they ask for—without a moment's hesitation, at least the next time they ask.

GET IT FOR FREE

(OR RIDICULOUSLY CHEAP)

MOVING BOXES

There's no reason to purchase moving boxes. You can find clean, quality boxes for free near the loading docks of liquor and computer stores. You can ask friends and neighbors who have recently moved for their used boxes. You could also post an ad requesting used boxes on Craigslist or Freecycle; or try www.hribar.com/free-moving-boxes.html, a real estate Web site that offers a free moving box exchange listing service. There's also usedcardboardboxes.com, which collects boxes from people who have recently moved and sells them inexpensively to people who need them.

Saving Money on Professional Movers

If you're hiring movers, there are good ways to save money—and bad ways. Do not try to pinch pennies by choosing a company that gives you a lowball price; the moving industry is notoriously full of shady companies just waiting to scam you. They might do this by jacking up the price by thousands of dollars after every one of your possessions is loaded on their truck, by showing up at your new house weeks after the promised arrival date, or by stealing your belongings. So step one is to choose a reputable moving company, and step two is to look for safe ways to cut costs.

Choosing a Reputable Mover

- Don't find your movers by going to a Web site that offers bids from multiple moving companies. Instead, get references from friends who have moved recently. You can also log on to the Web site of the American Moving and Storage Association, www.moving.org, and click on "Find a CMC" for a list of local movers that are certified by the trade group.

- Check out the companies' track records by calling your local Better Business Bureau (which you can locate at www.bbb.org) or by clicking on "The Black List" at www.movingscam.com (which also offer lots of useful tips about hiring movers). You can also get a list of state agencies that regulate movers from the Federal Motor Carrier Safety Administration (www.fmcsa.dot.gov).

- Ask for long lists of references from a few companies that haven't been red-flagged by your research, and then call a random sampling of those references to find out how the former clients' moves went.

- Get a walk-through. A representative of the moving company should come to your home to see what needs to be moved and thus estimate a fee based on an accurate assessment of the volume of your belongings as well as any other special situations (awkward staircases, especially fragile items, and the like), along with the number of miles you'll be moving, of course. Otherwise, you may be in for a higher-than-expected bill when the movers show up and assess the move for the first time.

- Get a binding bid. The bid should be in writing and should be a final or maximum price, not an estimate. And it should state that if something arises on the day of the move that warrants an increase in that price— perhaps you remember that big stash of gear in the basement storage locker that you forgot to mention during the walk through, or you realize that you need to swing by a friend's house to drop off some furniture that won't be moved into your new home—the mover will give you the additional price in writing before the move. (This is designed to avoid the biggest con job in the moving business—when the mover jacks up the price claiming that the job is bigger than anticipated and holds your stuff hostage until you pay up in cash.)

- Buy the moving company's insurance—or purchase a policy through www.movinginsurance.com.

Keep Costs Down

- Get rid of things you really don't need before you move. Donate old clothing to a charity (make sure you get a receipt for tax purposes, of course), toss out broken lawn furniture, and consider not bringing that old behemoth fridge you'd been planning on putting in the new garage for chilling beer.

- If you have some flexibility in your time line, you may be able to negotiate a lower price by avoiding the first of the month by a few days; by avoiding June or September, the two biggest moving months (thanks to college schedules); and, for long-haul moves, by letting the movers deliver your belongings when it works best for their schedule.

- Do your own packing. Not only will this lower the movers' labor charges, but you won't have to pay them for packing materials, for which they charge a premium.

- Move some of your belongings yourself. If you specify this stuff to the salesman who comes to bid on the job, it'll reduce your price. Plus, it gives you a chance to handle fragile items (like artwork), valuable items (such as electronics), and odd-size items (like plants) yourself.

- For heavy boxed objects, such as books, you may get a better price from the post office for shipping them parcel post than you'll get from a mover. Take a sample box to the post office for a weigh-in and a price, then compare this with your mover's fee (which is generally quoted per pound).

- Or you can skip the professionals entirely and put together your own moving team by paying college students by the hour for their labor. Post ads on campus or on Craigslist. Even if you have to pay a couple of guys $15 or $20 an hour, you'll spend a lot less than you would for a professional mover.

THE CATCH You'll have to do the move with them to orchestrate things. }

REFINISHING FLOORS AND PAINTING WALLS BEFORE YOU MOVE IN

By far the best time to paint walls and refinish floors is when the house is empty. So if you can swing the investment—and the timing—it's a great idea to take care of these jobs before moving day.

You can write off the costs of moving (a professional mover's fee, if you hired one; packing materials; mileage driven; truck rental; insurance; and even pizza and beer for your helpers) if your move meets three IRS criteria:

1. You're moving within one year of starting a new job—and the new home is closer to your job than your old home.

2. Your new job is 50 miles farther from your old home than your previous job.

3. Your new job is a full-time position.

Talk to a tax adviser about whether you qualify, because there are exceptions to these rules.

{ HOUSE MONEY: }
DOLLARS AND SENSE FOR
HOUSEHOLD FINANCES

Why is there so much month left at
the end of the money?

—Anonymous

Managing your money isn't nearly as much fun as decorating and furnishing your home—but focusing a little energy on your monthly finances will ensure that you have the biggest possible home improvement budget, that you don't waste money on junk bank and credit fees, and that you'll qualify for the best available interest rates when you need a loan someday.

5 WAYS TO BE SMART ABOUT YOUR MONEY

No matter how much—or how little—money you make, if you can live by these five rules, your finances will always be healthy.

1. Stay on top of your credit card spending. Forget the fact that credit cards are actually loans, and pay off your entire balance every month. If you ever need to break this rule because of a financial emergency, make sure to pay more than the minimum balance (which is calculated to increase your debt rather than reduce it from one month to the next), and always get your payment in by the due date. Also, consider transferring the balance to a zero-interest card (see "Free Money" in this chapter).

2. Build up some savings. Establish an automatic monthly transfer into a high-interest savings account (such as the ones at EmigrantDirect.com) to build a cushion that will help you through unforeseen expenses. No ifs, ands, or buts. Just do it, even if all you can afford to contribute is $25 per month.

3. Fund your 401(k), if you have one. With all Social Security's troubles, it's likely that your own savings will be the only money you'll have for retire-

ment. That's why financial advisers recommend kicking in at least 10 percent of your annual salary each year, but it's okay if you can't meet that goal right after buying a home. Do put in as much as you need to, however, to ensure that your employer will contribute the maximum matching amount that it offers. (For example, some employers match 50 cents on the dollar up to 6 percent in employee contributions. In that case, contributing any less than 6 percent is like throwing away part of your compensation.)

4. Play at home. Learn to cook, to mix blender drinks, and to socialize at home instead of at the local pub or nightclub. This can save you hundreds of dollars per month—and give you a chance to show off your great new house, too. Also, host potluck dinners, board-game parties, and movie nights. (You can swap DVDs for free on TitleTrader.com, check them out of the library, or rent them cheaply from Netflix.com.)

5. Manage your money. Keep track of your finances with a computer program and you'll avoid fees from missed or late payments and overdrafts. Also, save your receipts (see "What Financial Documents Should You Save?" in this chapter). That way you can write off all the costs of your home office, if you have one; you'll have the ammunition to prove when you've been overcharged for something; and you'll be ready for any IRS audit that comes your way.

SHARING COSTS

If you're sharing your home with other people, you need to decide how you'll share your various housing costs, too. The best way to do that depends on whom you're living with.

Roommates

It's a good idea to come to an agreement about the ground rules right at the start. Decide what costs are going to be shared—such as rent, utilities, cleaning person, or shared food items. (You can include the phone bill, too, but sorting out whose long-distance calls are whose can be a frustration, so consider having each resi-

dent use her own cell phone for long-distance calls.) Then appoint the household's most anal-retentive member to tally the bills each month and divide them evenly among the roommates. It's a thankless job, so consider giving a small discount on the monthly bills (or chores) to the person who does it.

Couples

Adding all the bills and then splitting them down the middle isn't very romantic. So consider splitting the big stuff like rent and heat, then just alternate who pays which small bill. Or, if you're testing the waters for spending your lives together, think about opening a joint household account from which you pay all your bills. Keep your own accounts, too, and share the cost of funding the joint account— either down the middle or possibly at some other ratio if one person makes a lot more money than the other.

Spouses

You're married now, so combine your finances into one joint checking account, eliminate the personal accounts, and simplify your life. Doing so may feel scary at first, especially if one spouse makes a lot more money than the other or you each have very different spending habits, but combining accounts cuts down on the time it takes to manage the household bills. It also makes you true partners in the household—and the relationship.

THE CATCH Don't do this if one spouse has bad credit. In this case you'll want to keep your finances totally separate to avoid driving down the other person's credit rating by association. }

■ WORTH THE MONEY

QUICKEN

When it comes to household finances, nothing is as important as keeping your checkbook balanced and getting your bills paid on time—otherwise you'll have to shell out all sorts of money for fees, penalties, and high interest rates simply because you're disorganized. Luckily, there's an easy way to keep your accounts balanced and up to date—Quicken. This software puts your financial "books" onto your computer. You enter information about checks you write, charges you make on your credit card, and your direct deposit from work, and it'll automatically do the math. It'll also track your spending, help you prepare your taxes, and let you know whether you're staying within your budget. And don't worry: Keying in your information is simple, because the program automatically recognizes repeat transactions, filling in the information so you don't have to. You may also be able to download transaction data into Quicken directly from the Web sites of your bank and credit cards.

THE TAXMAN COMETH

Congratulations, you own a home now. Your taxes just got a lot more complicated. The bad news is that you're now going to have to pay thousands of dollars a year in property taxes. The good news is you'll also get a big drop in your federal income taxes.

How Your Home Can Cut Your Income Taxes

Homeownership, whether you're in a house, condo, or co-op, can give you a windfall on your tax returns. Here's how to make the most of it:

- The main tax advantage to homeownership, of course, is that mortgage interest is deductible. You can maximize your mortgage interest deduction for the current tax year by paying your January bill in December.

That way the interest you pay for that January bill will count in the current tax year.

- If you paid points to the bank to get a lower mortgage interest rate, that money is deductible, too, in the year you bought your home. (Points paid for refinancing are not deductible, however.)

- Because you have mortgage interest to write off now, you'll have enough write-offs to warrant itemizing your deductions on your tax forms. This means you can add in a whole host of other deductible expenses that you couldn't when using the standard deduction. So make sure to save receipts for medical costs, child care, job searches, property taxes paid, job-related moving expenses, uniform costs, cash donations to charities, clothing given to charities, books donated to libraries, magazines donating to nursing homes (libraries don't want magazines, but many nursing homes do), business expenses, and anything else that's tax deductible. (Consult a tax adviser about what write-offs you qualify for.)

  THE CATCH You won't be able to use the EZ form anymore. }

- If you work at home, you may be able to take a deduction for a home office as well. You'll need an expert's take on whether your office qualifies, but in general it will if it's your sole place of business and the space is dedicated entirely to your work. If so, you can write off a portion of your home expenses—from utility bills to the cleaning person to home maintenance costs—that's equivalent to the proportion of the home's square footage taken up by the office. (Thus a 150-square-foot office in a 1,000-square-foot home translates into writing off 15 percent of many routine home expenses.)

- Owning a home also qualifies you for home equity loans—for which you can write off the interest that you pay, no matter what you use the money for. Just watch out for the potential pitfalls of home equity borrowing (see "The Lowdown on Borrowing" in this chapter).

Fighting Property Tax Hikes

Every now and then the city or town where you live is going to reassess all the houses within its borders. These new assessments—which may take place shortly after you purchase the house or on a regular cycle, such as every three years, depending on your state's law—will be the basis for your future tax bills, so just what your house is assessed at will have a big impact on your property taxes. (Don't worry, your taxes won't go up proportionally to your new assessment. After a revaluation, the town's mill rate—the tax rate—typically drops proportionally to the average increase in house values.)

The good news is that—because the methods used to value the properties are subjective and imprecise—there's an appeals process whereby homeowners can challenge their assessments. And it's well worth appealing, since about half of all homeowners who do wind up getting a reduction. You don't need a lawyer; you just need to check your revaluation paperwork to see what the appeals process is, and then to build your case. Look at your assessment carefully to see whether there are any errors, such as a typo that accidentally credits you with having half an acre instead of a quarter acre or with having an extra bathroom or a two-car garage that simply doesn't exist. Bring proof that the data is wrong to the hearing and they're likely to correct the problem right there on the spot.

If you don't find any glaring errors, you'll need to argue that your assessment is unfair. And to do that, you need to review the assessments of your immediate neighbors, which are available for review at town hall, and often on the Web. Look for comparable homes—those of similar size and with similar features—to see what they're assessed for. If a house that's virtually identical to yours in every way was assessed for less than yours, or one like yours but with an in-ground pool or a large addition isn't assessed above yours, bring the documentation to your hearing. And don't worry—the hearings aren't adversarial. Tax officials want to be evenhanded, so if you can show them that they haven't been, they'll correct the problem. And if you can't, you haven't lost a thing—except perhaps a nonrefundable $5 to $25 appeal filing fee in some states.

GET PAID TO VOLUNTEER

Do you volunteer at the local library, soup kitchen, animal shelter, or Big Brother/Big Sister organization? If you donate your time to any nonprofit charity, make sure to record your mileage driving to and from the location—those miles are tax deductible. Meals and overnight lodging associated with volunteering far from home may be deductible as well.

Free Help with Your Taxes

If you're struggling with your tax forms and would like some expert help, you don't necessarily have to hire a CPA—or a tax preparation store. You can get free assistance from a number of sources:

- **The IRS.** The Internal Revenue Service offers tax-filing assistance at its branch offices, which you can locate by clicking "Contact My Local Office" on the www.irs.gov Web site.

  THE CATCH These guys play things totally by the book, so no fudging—make sure you have sufficient documentation for any borderline claims.

- **The AARP.** From February 1 through April 15 each year, this association of retired people offers free tax help at numerous locations in every state. And although the service is geared toward AARP members, it's open to nonmembers of all ages. The group also offers free answers to tax questions year-round on its Web site. To access the Q&A portion of the site or to find a tax assistance office near you, go to www.aarp.org and search for "Tax-Aide."

- **SnapTax.** This free service is provided by the makers of the tax preparation software TurboTax as a way to promote their software. And such software certainly isn't a bad idea—it will simplify the process of filing your taxes. Whether you buy the software or not, however, you can get the free help at www.snaptax.com.

- **Schools.** Some college and university cooperative extension services offer free tax assistance. Contact your nearest university's main office and ask about extension services in your area.

- **Unions, credit unions, and libraries.** If you're a member of a union or a credit union, that organization may offer free tax help. You can also ask at your local library to see whether it has a similar program, or whether the librarians know of other local organizations that do.

WHAT FINANCIAL DOCUMENTS SHOULD YOU SAVE?

Stashing all of your important paperwork in a cardboard box isn't good enough. Okay, it is a step ahead of just throwing everything away, but you really need to keep your vital documents safe, secure, and sorted so they're always accessible when you need them.

Keep Forever in a Fireproof Safe or (Better) Safe-Deposit Box

- Birth certificate.

- Diplomas.

- Marriage and divorce certificates.

- Health records.

- Court documents.

- Up-to-date inventory and photos of household possessions.

- Records of military service, adoption, citizenship, or naturalization.

- Pension documents.

Keep for Seven Years in a Locked Filing Cabinet

- Bank statements.

- Canceled checks.

- Credit card statements.

- Tax returns and supporting documents.

- Loan agreements (until seven years after loan is paid off).

- Investment account statements.

- Home office and home business receipts (including improvement costs, which should be kept until seven years after selling the house).

Keep all other receipts financial documents at least until you've filed your tax return for that year.

■ DON'T WASTE YOUR MONEY ON

...TAX REFUND ANTICIPATION LOANS.

The loans are offered by tax preparation companies such as H&R Block and Jackson Hewitt, and they're marketed as a way to walk out of your tax prep appointment with your refund already in hand. Sounds great because you don't have to wait for Uncle Sam to send you a check, right? But these services are actually nothing more than loans—with fees so high that they make credit cards look like bargains. You're much better off waiting for your refund to come directly from the government.

SMART BANKING

Once upon a time, people actually went to the bank—frequently. Depositing pay-checks, withdrawing cash, and making account transfers or balance inquiries required walking into the local branch and waiting in line. And although innovations like bank machines and direct deposit have made the process faster and more convenient, choosing the right bank and being smart about how you use it has never been so important. Otherwise, high fees and low interest rates will skim big money out of your account.

5 Reasons to Pay Your Bills Online

Are you still writing checks? If so, you're living in the Dark Ages—and wasting money. Online bill paying is as easy as logging on to the Web site of the company that sent you the bill—or in many cases simply logging on to your bank's Web site, which is easier because it's one-stop shopping for all your bill paying—and signing up! Here's why paying online is better than putting a check in the mail:

1. You'll never miss a payment due date. Go online when you get the bill and schedule a payment. You can pick the day that the money gets transferred. No need to time the postal service—and no chance of a late payment. (Many banks even guarantee that the transfer will happen on time, or they'll cover the late fees.)

   > **THE CATCH** In a few rare cases, the bank may not be able to do a direct transfer to the payee and instead will have to issue an actual printed check, meaning you'll need to schedule the payment at least five business days before it's due.

2. You'll never pay a bill before it's due, either. Because you can pick the date that the money gets transferred, you can make sure that your money doesn't arrive a single day before it has to.

3. You'll save on stamps. Online bill paying is free, while sending a check through the mail costs money—and the cost of a stamp keeps going up.

4. You'll save on check-printing fees. It'll be a very long time before you have to order new checks if you pay all your credit card, utility, and loan bills online.

5. You'll save time. The first time you pay a bill online, you'll have to key in some account information, but the next time it'll take only a few key-strokes to pay—and it can be done in less than a third of the time it takes to write and mail a check.

How to Avoid Rip-Off Fees from Banks

The idea that a bank would charge its account holders a single dime is a travesty of justice. After all, the bank invests the money that you deposit and reaps the profits for itself (passing along only a tiny portion—if any—back to you in interest). And yet many banks charge their customers big monthly fees unless they keep a high minimum balance, which means you're giving them even more money to invest. On top of that, anytime you use a "foreign" ATM—one at another bank—both your bank and the one that owns the ATM may charge your account from $1 to $3, even though automated tellers actually save banks a lot of money as compared with human ones.

Luckily, it doesn't have to be that way. To avoid spending hundreds of dollars a year in junk bank fees, you can:

• Shop around for a bank that offers free checking. If you use the ATM fre-quently, make sure to choose an institution with machines in convenient locations near home and work. Better yet, choose one of the growing number of small banks that actually waives ATM surcharges—and covers foreign institutions' fees as well—so that you can use any ATM for free.

• Track your finances with a program such as Quicken. And create an Internet login for your bank account so that you can keep close tabs on your balances and make any necessary transfers 24/7 in order to avoid overdrafts, for which banks typically charge high fees.

• Pay your bills online to reduce the number of checks you'll need to buy.

• When you do need checks, don't order them through your bank's printing service. You'll pay a fraction of the cost by getting them from a discounter such as Checks In the Mail (http://secure.checksinthemail.com).

E-Bank Bargains

Banks pay pitifully low interest rates these days on savings and money market accounts. But putting anything other than long-term savings into mutual funds is too risky. So what should you do with your money? No, don't stash it under your mattress—put it in an Internet savings account. These virtual banks offer interest rates that may be double or triple what you'll get from your local institution—and your money is just as safe because these e-banks are covered by the FDIC. There are no fees or minimum balances for the accounts, and your money is totally liquid, which means you can withdraw it anytime you like. You simply open an account online, and then link it to your checking account. All deposits and withdrawals are then done online.

THE CATCH Transfers take a few days to clear, so don't wait until the last minute to shift funds that you need. }

Here are a few leading e-banks:

- EmigrantDirect.com (www.emigrantdirect.com).

- HSBC Bank (www.hsbcdirect.com).

- Ing Bank (www.ingdirect.com).

To see a list of which banks are offering the highest rates on any given day, visit www.bankrate.com.

CREDIT WHERE CREDIT IS DUE

The credit card industry keeps coming up with ever more generous ways to attract new customers—and soak them. For every promotional deal there's a mile of fine print loaded with traps designed to snare you into owing fees and interest. Still, if you're exacting about following a few basic rules, and you don't overuse your cards, you can reap a big harvest of cash from these offers.

Free Money

Need a little extra money to get started in the house? Want to amortize a big purchase over a few months, rather than paying for it all at once? Carrying a few thousand bucks in credit card debt that's costing you a lot of money in interest and fees?

If you answered yes to any of these questions, there is a way to borrow the money you need for twelve to eighteen months—and pay not so much as a dime in interest or fees. But this technique, which is called card surfing, is not for everyone. You need to have good credit to qualify—and you need to be absolutely exacting about the procedure to avoid falling into numerous traps designed to hit you with huge fees. So go surfing only if you always (always!) pay your bills like clockwork and there's no risk that you'll miss a single payment.

Charge the purchases you're looking to float using a regular credit card, then use the following procedure to transfer the balance before the bill comes due:

1. Go to www.cardratings.com, which is a credit card review site where you can search through all the available card deals. Look for a credit card that's offering 0 percent interest for twelve or more months on balance transfers. Make sure there's no balance transfer fee.

2. Apply for the new card either online or by phone, and as part of the process provide the necessary information to have your existing credit card balance transferred to the new card.

3. Mark the expiration date of the 0 percent deal on your calendar—or better yet, subtract a few weeks and mark that down as the expiration date, just to give yourself a little cushion.

4. Do not use your new card for any new purchases or balance transfers not included in the special introductory offer. (If you do, the payment systems are set up so that you cannot pay back the new debt until the entire transferred balance is paid off, which means you'll get creamed with high interest costs and fees.) Just continue to use your old card for future purchases.

5. Pay at least the minimum balance by the due date without fail every month. Making one mistake can invalidate the special offer and hit you with enormous interest fees.

6. Set up a payment schedule that will have the entire balance paid off before the expiration date comes along—or transfer the remaining balance to another introductory-rate card before it does.

THE CATCH Opening too many new cards can lower your credit rating; don't open more than one or two new accounts each year. }

Cards That Pay You Back

Here's another way that you can beat the credit card system, as long as you have good credit and are scrupulous about paying off your entire credit card balance by the due date every month: Sign up for a rewards card that gives you something back for every purchase you make. You can earn anything from discounts on vacations to free cups of coffee, but most of the best deals involve cold cash. A sampling of what was available at the time of this writing includes cards with no annual fee that:

- Pay you 3 percent cash back for all purchases at supermarkets, drugstores, and gas stations plus 1 percent back on all other purchases with up to $500 in rewards per year.

- Give you 1.5 percent back for all purchases, which will be transferred into a linked investment or savings account, with no annual reward cap.

- Give you 1 percent back for all purchases, which automatically gets credited toward paying down your mortgage, with no annual reward cap.

- Earn 1 frequent flier mile for every dollar spent using the card, plus 1 mile for every 1.5 miles flown on any airline if the tickets were purchased using the card (in addition to the airline's own frequent flier program). About 25,000 miles can be redeemed for a free domestic flight on any airline.

> **THE CATCH** The interest on rewards cards is typically 1 percentage point higher than other cards, which can easily cost you more than you earn in rewards, so always pay off the entire monthly balance.

To find the best deals available, go to www.cardratings.com.

The Truth about Debit Cards

In an effort to control the temptation to spend spend spend with credit cards, many people now carry debit cards instead. These MasterCards and Visas operate just like credit cards, except the money is automatically transferred from your checking account instead of being billed to a credit card account. There's no risk of spending your way into a huge credit card bill, since you can only spend the money you have in your checking account. Still, there are some major drawbacks to debit cards:

- If someone steals your credit card and racks up a huge bill, by law you are responsible for only $50 of the charges (and some issuers extend this to $0). With a debit card, there's no such law, so you could be out of luck if a thief clears out your checking account and creates a host of overdraft fees to boot. Most debit card issuers do offer a $50 or $0 liability policy, but the fine print usually states that it's valid only if you report the problem within forty-eight hours of the initial theft.

- A debit card won't help you build a history of good credit, which is essential for getting the best available rates on future car loans, home equity loans, and mortgages.

- In case of emergency, a debit card can't be used to pay for large expenses, unless you have enough money in your checking account to cover the bill.

- Most rental car agencies won't accept debit cards for renting a vehicle.

- Debit purchases don't always post right away. So unless you're scrupulous about monitoring your spending (rather than just checking your daily balances), it's easy to assume you have more money than you really do—and thus overdraw your account.

What You Need to Know about Credit Ratings

You can save yourself a lot of money on future car loans, mortgages, and home equity lines of credit by being smart with your credit cards now. That's because anytime you apply for credit, the company checks your credit score, which is a computer-generated rating (from 300 to 850) of your credit risk based on your credit history. Here are the primary ways that the number is generated:

- Payment history (35 percent). Just paying your bills on time will go a long way toward keeping your score healthy. And the easiest way to ensure that you always make the due date is to pay your bills online. When the bill arrives, log on to the Web site of your bank or the creditor and schedule a payment, to arrive right on the due date if you like.

- Amounts owed (30 percent). Obviously, owing less money makes your financial picture look healthier, but not so obviously, this is analyzed by comparing how much you owe with how much credit you have available. So don't close old credit card accounts or lines of credit that you no longer use. You're better off simply shredding the card so you continue to get the benefit of its unused credit limit, without the risk of someone stealing it.

- Length of credit history (15 percent). The longer your history, the better. This is another reason not to close old accounts—especially those cards that you've had for a long time.

- New credit (10 percent). Every time you apply for credit, on the other hand, your score goes down a few points, so resist the urge to open credit cards at your favorite clothing store in order to get a discount on your purchases that day. As a general rule, you shouldn't fill out more than one or two credit applications each year. Save those applications for card surfing (see "Free Money" in this chapter) or generous rewards cards rather than store cards, which tend to offer stingy rewards and high interest rates.

PROTECTING YOUR IDENTITY

Identity theft gets a lot of newspaper ink these days, from national headlines to small-town police blotters. Yet most people don't fully understand what identity theft is or how to protect themselves.

What Identity Theft Is

The most common type of identity theft is when someone steals your credit card number and racks up a bunch of debt in your name. The thief can be a store clerk to whom you give your information, an old-fashioned crook who gets a look inside your wallet or filing cabinet, or someone who sends out fraudulent e-mails pretending to be your bank and asking for personal information about your account. Having your credit card number stolen is scary and can lead to a lot of angst, but the truth is that the federal government requires credit card companies to absolve their customers of all but $50 in fraudulent spending. Thus there's not much financial risk if you have your credit card stolen (there is no such legal protection for debit cards, however; see "The Truth About Debit Cards" in this chapter).

But there is another kind of identity theft that can cause a lot more harm. Rather than stealing your credit card information, thieves can steal your name, Social Security number, birthday, and address—the sort of information that you regularly fill out on all sorts of forms and that can be found in your mailbox or garbage can—and use it to actually adopt your identity. The thief can then take out her own credit cards, rent an apartment, open a bank account, get a job, sign up for cell phone service, or anything else she wants to do, all in your name. She might rack up tens of thousands of dollars in unpaid debt. Or she may pay her bills on time for a while because she's using your identity to hide from immigration officials, child support payments, parole officers, or whoever else may be after her.

What It Does

Victims of the latter, scarier kind of identity theft experience everything from destroyed credit ratings to being arrested for crimes committed by someone using their name. All these problems eventually get sorted out, of course, but only after weeks, months, and sometimes years of dealing with untrusting customer service agents, bureaucratic red tape at credit bureaus, and occasionally court dates.

How to Protect Yourself

The unfortunate reality is that there's not much you can do to prevent identity theft, other than taking some basic steps to protect your personal information: Don't leave your purse in your unlocked car, shred any documents that include personal information before throwing them away, and never provide personal information by e-mail or over the phone unless you've initiated contact. Also, don't use obvious passwords—birthdays, zip codes—for ATM cards and other accounts.

Beyond that, your best protection against identity theft is to catch it early, before too much damage has been done. And that means regularly checking your credit rating (don't pay a service to do it for you; see "Get It for Free" in this chapter). For more information about identity theft, go to www.consumer.gov/idtheft or www.idtheftcenter.org.

THE LOWDOWN ON BORROWING

Here's what you need to know about loans—and where to get the best deals on them.

Car Loans

If you're buying a new car, chances are good that the dealer will have the best interest rates in town—but don't count on it. Always walk in with a loan already secured. If the dealer beats what you already have in your back pocket, take the dealer's offer. If not, use your backup loan so you're not stuck. The best place to go for that backup loan—or a used-car loan—is a credit union, because they have the lowest rates around. And many credit unions are open to all comers. To see a list of credit unions, go to www.cuna.org. Also, consider using a home equity loan as your backup for a car purchase, since the rate will be lower and the interest you pay will be tax deductible.

Home Equity Loans

These loans use the equity you have in your home as collateral, which means you'll get a much better interest rate than you can for standard personal loans or auto loans. Plus, thanks to a tax loophole, you can write off the interest you pay on these loans just like mortgage interest, no matter what you use the borrowed money for.

You can get a home equity loan for a fixed amount of money at a fixed interest rate, or you can take a line of credit, which is like a credit card that you can spend as you need it. That flexibility, plus the often lower initial interest rates of these adjustable-rate lines of credit, make them very popular, but they have some of the same credit traps as regular credit cards. In particular, if you pay only the minimum balance, your debt will grow rather than shrink each month. So you need to establish your own repayment schedule—say, five years for a car purchase or ten for a major remodeling project—and stick with it.

For both home equity loans and lines of credit, you'll likely get the best deals from local banks, especially small savings banks, which need to have great deals to compete with the better-known regional and national brand banks all around them. And for lines of credit, don't make the mistake of judging the loan by its current interest rate—which will change every year. What really matters is how the annual rate will be determined. These rates are calculated based on the prime rate, which is simply a fluctuating rate that all banks use as an industry standard. For example, you might find a line at prime, at prime plus 0.5 percentage point, or perhaps even at 1 percentage point below prime, which is obviously your best choice among these examples.

Cash-Out Refinancing

Always popular when interest rates are falling, cash-out refinancing allows you to basically exchange your old mortgage for a new one. Along the way you can cash out some of your equity. In some cases your monthly payment can actually decrease after refinancing, but remember that you're restarting the loan cycle, which means you'll be paying almost solely interest again until you get a few years into the new loan. Plus, since the new loan will have a new thirty-year term, refinancing means you're moving farther from the day when you'll own your house outright—an important financial goal to reach before you retire, when you won't want to have a mortgage payment to worry about. Also, the money that you cash out amounts to a thirty-year loan. That's a long time—and a lot of interest—to pay for a car or whatever you're buying with the money.

If you choose the refinance route, local banks typically have the best rates, and also far lower closing costs than mortgage brokers. A fixed-rate mortgage is generally the safest option—unless you're sure you'll be moving in the near future, in which case you might consider an adjustable rate that starts with a fixed term for five, seven, or ten years. Aim for a fixed introductory rate that lasts at least as long as you intend to live in the house.

Should You Prepay Your Mortgage?

Prepaying your mortgage—paying a little extra principal with every payment, or whenever you have some extra cash—can save you a lot of money over the course of a thirty-year loan. For example, on a typical mortgage, paying an extra $100 every month could save you $63,000 in interest over the life of the loan and knock the thirty-year term down to about twenty-four. Even just a onetime extra payment of $1,000 in the second year of your loan could save you $6,000 in interest—and half a year—over the life of the loan.

Still, prepaying isn't always the best move. Stashing the extra cash in an Internet savings account (see "E-Bank Bargains" in this chapter) is likely to give you a better return on the money if you have a low mortgage rate. Here's how to determine whether it will:

1. Look up your adjusted gross income (AGI) on last year's tax return. (This is your income after it's combined with your spouse's, if you have one, and with all deductions taken out.)

2. Go to www.irs.gov and enter tax rate schedules in the search box. Click on the results for the most recent tax year.

3. Find your AGI on the appropriate chart (for single or married filers, for example).

4. Determine your tax bracket. This is not your total tax percentage. Taxes are determined on a sliding scale; your bracket is the highest amount you pay. For example, in 2006 married couples paid 10 percent on their first $15,100 of income and then 15 percent on income between $15,100 and $61,300. So a married couple with a combined AGI of, say, $50,000 was in the 15 percent bracket.

5. Go to your state tax department's Web site and follow the same procedure for figuring out your state tax bracket. (Some states have a flat tax percentage for everyone.)

6. Add your federal and state brackets together. A couple in the 15 percent federal bracket and 6 percent state bracket would be at 21 percent total.

7. Subtract that number from 100 (100 – 21 = 79, in our example).

8. Multiply the result by your mortgage interest rate (79 x 6 percent, let's say).

9. The result is your effective mortgage interest rate after the tax deduction (4.74 percent in our example).

Compare that rate with what's being offered by Internet savings banks or other institutions to see which will give you a bigger payback. And keep in mind one key advantage that's always true of the savings account option: The money will be accessible if you need it later. Once you deposit it into your mortgage account, however, you can't get it back (other than by taking a home equity loan or cash-out refinancing).

SLASHING YOUR INSURANCE BILL

Paying for insurance really sucks. It's expensive, you're hoping that you'll never have to make a claim, and to add insult to injury, if you do wind up making a claim or two, your insurance company may raise your rates or even cancel your coverage. Still, insurance is an important safeguard against the potentially enormous costs of large accidents and disasters. And there are some ways that you can keep your premiums low:

• Choose the right type of coverage. You don't need life insurance until you have children (at which point you'll want term life, which is the cheapest alternative). You do need homeowner's insurance now, however, even if you're a renter, in which case you'll be purchasing only the portion of the policy that covers the belongings contained in the house. And if you have a car, you'll also need car insurance, of course.

- Skip the agent. Since insurance agents typically take a 15 percent cut for themselves, you'll almost always get a better price by buying from a direct seller. And the best direct sellers—such as Amica (800-242-6422, www.amica.com), Erie Insurance (800-458-0811, www.erieinsurance.com), GEICO (800-861-8380, www.geico.com), and USAA (open only to members and veterans of the military and their families; 800-531-8080, www.usaa.com)—provide better customer service than you'll get from most agents anyway.

- Buy quality. Here's one time when you don't want to choose your provider based solely on price. You want to make sure that you're dealing with a reliable company that's actually going to come through if and when you need to file a claim. To see quality ratings of insurance companies, go to www.ambest.com, www.jdpower.com, and www.naic.org.

- Combine policies. Buying both car and homeowner's insurance from the same company is usually good for a 5 to 15 percent discount on your homeowner's policy.

- Raise your deductible. Increasing your car insurance deductible from $250 to $1,000 could save you $500 a year in premiums.

  THE CATCH

  In the event of a claim, you'll be on the hook for the first $1,000 before the coverage kicks in. Still, you'll save that much money in premiums in just a couple of years, so it's well worth the risk.

- Drive safely. In most states, going three years without a moving violation or insurance claim will win you a safe driver discount.

- Maintain good credit. Insurers give better rates to people with clean credit ratings, because they're statistically less likely to have accidents.

MONEY RESOURCES ON THE WEB

Most of what's on the Internet could just as well be printed on the page of a book or magazine. But there are some truly interactive sites, where you can plug in specific data and get back useful information that's tailored to your situation:

Realtor.com

In addition to offering a huge online listing of houses for sale, the National Association of Realtors' Web site has a great selection of home-buying-related calculators. Find out how much house you can afford, the financial pros and cons of buying versus renting, the relative costs of a fixed versus adjustable mortgage rate, and much more.

Edmunds.com

A great resource for analyzing the fair price of new and used cars before making your deal, this site also offers some useful calculators. You can compare the costs of buying versus leasing, for example, or choose whether to take cash back or a low interest rate from the dealer.

Zillow.com

Enter almost any street address and find out what features the house has, and what this Web site's supercomputer thinks a fair selling price would be.

Bankrate.com

Get up-to-the-minute numbers for the best rates on credit cards, mortgages, car loans, and a lot more.

Hughchou.org

This blog has dozens of useful calculators about everything from retirement planning to tax planning. It also has some very handy ones for figuring out the price of little expenses that really add up. For example, did you know that drinking the less-than-perfect coffee served for free in your office will save you about $10,000 over the course of the next decade as compared with buying a cup of Starbucks every weekday morning? Or how much you'll save over the years by bringing a brown-bag lunch, buying a fuel-efficient vehicle, or quitting smoking?

SHOP RIGHT

No self-respecting Cheap Bastard wants to pay full retail price. So, you probably haggle with the used-car dealer and the neighbor holding a tag sale. But do you nonetheless blithely pay asking price at retail stores and Web sites because you assume there's no flexibility in the price? Don't lose out on an opportunity to save! Here's how to score a bargain on whatever you're buying.

Negotiating 101

There is no more important money-saving skill than the ability to negotiate. Whether you're at the used-car lot or the flea market, you need to be firm without ever painting yourself into a corner. Here are some tricks for keeping the upper hand in any negotiation:

- Pick your battles. If you must have whatever it is you're buying, you don't have a lot of bargaining power, and the seller almost surely knows that. So there's little you can do beyond simply asking if he can do any better on the price. Also, it's generally not a good idea to push too hard in negotiating for someone's professional services (be it a housepainter or a car mechanic). If he agrees to a reduced rate, he's going to look for ways to cut corners on the work.

- Do your homework. You can use the Internet to determine the going rate for almost any product you buy, from used cars (www.edmunds.com or www.kbb.com) to household goods (check out the recent sale prices on similar items at www.ebay.com). And you can also refer to *The Garage Sale & Flea Market Annual* (Collector Books) for pricing guidelines. Mention the information you learn—and where you learned it—in your negotiation.

- Time it right. You're always going to get more flexibility from sellers when they're eager to unload the item. So, if possible, wait until the end of a farmers' market, late afternoon at a tag sale, or right after Christmas if you're buying something that's often purchased for gifts (such as jewelry). Walk into a car dealership in the late afternoon before a holiday weekend on the last business day of the month, because dealers have monthly sales quotas to fill, it'll be a slow sales time, and these folks want to go home.

- Make the second move. Begin any negotiation by asking the other person to give you her best price. (The asking price on a car-window sticker or a store price tag doesn't count.) Then you can make a counteroffer and push her even farther.

- Relax. If you're negotiating in person, allow silences to happen in the conversation. There's nothing like a pregnant pause to get the other person to start babbling or lowering the price. If you're negotiating by e-mail, take at least a few hours to reply to your opponent's e-mails.

- Anticipate the middle ground. Decide what your maximum price is before you start the negotiation. Then, since good negotiations often meet in the middle, make your first offer low enough that you're prepared to come up to the middle to make a deal. In other words, if a desk is marked at $150 at a flea market, and you feel that $125 is fair, make your first offer at $100.

- Be prepared to walk. If you can't get the seller to come down to the maximum price you're willing to pay, thank him for his time and move on. There's always a chance that he'll chase you down and take your last offer, but that's not what you're counting on. It's your willingness to walk away that ensures that you won't overpay for the item, after all. (On the other hand, there's nothing wrong with "losing" a negotiation if you're still getting good deal on an item you really want.)

Trading Online

Don't buy anything without first checking the following sources, where you may be able to get it at an amazingly low price—or even for free:

Craigslist.org

What began as a free Web site for events listings and classified advertisements in San Francisco now has sites in all fifty states and thirty-five countries. There is no charge to post ads—except for help wanted ads—and so people list almost anything you could possibly want, from apartments to bongo drums to kittens.

Freecycle.org

Started by environmentalists as an effort to promote recycling, this Web site links to regional communities across the country. Join up and you'll see dozens of free items that your neighbors are looking to pass along to someone else. Everything is free, and shipping is discouraged in favor of personal handoffs.

SwapThing.com

This site provides a forum for swapping things you don't want for things you do. Join up and you can see what other members are offering, and suggest trades for things you're looking to get rid of. The site charges $1 per trade, no matter what is being exchanged, and collects via a PayPal account (see "eBay Know-How" in this chapter).

Swapstyle.com

Join an online swap meet dedicated to fashion, where you can browse other people's wardrobes and get their unwanted items, sometimes for free, sometimes for a small price, and sometimes in exchange for a piece of your own unwanted clothing or accessories.

TheFreeSite.com and FreebieDirectory.com

These sites link to hundreds of others where you can get free product samples from major corporations (especially pharmacy products such as shaving supplies and condoms); enter free sweepstakes (for all sorts of monetary prizes); and download free computer software (graphics, games, sounds).

THE CATCH You're going to have to provide your name, e-mail, and mailing address to sign up for the freebies (which will definitely increase your future junk mail, both virtual and electronic); you may have to fill out numerous online surveys; and some sites charge for shipping the freebies to you.

Overstock.com

You can't beat the prices at this online clearance store, which sells products that manufacturers are looking to unload because they've overproduced them or are replacing the models with something new. As a result, you can find markdowns of 40 to 80 percent on many useful products.

Buy.com

This virtual megamart has the volume of a big box store but a lot less overhead, so check its prices before you buy just about any easily shipped product.

Freegan.info

Freegans live outside the conventional economy—avoiding consumerism, car own-ership, animal products, the eighty-hour workweek, and anything disposable. They also sponsor "Really Free Markets," which are part swap meet and part festival. Check the Web site for upcoming Really Free Markets around the country. You never know what you'll find at a freegan market, but plants, artwork, clothing, and books are the most common items. And you probably won't see anything larger than what you can carry off in your hands. There's no need to bring something in order to take something, but do make sure to bring a tote bag to collect your finds.

Tax-Free Shopping

Along with the convenience of shopping anytime day or night and doing it from the comfort of your own home, one big perk of online shopping is that you often don't have to pay sales tax.

Currently, e-tailers must collect sales tax from you only if they have a brick-and-mortar presence in your state. So national chains with numerous storefronts wind up collecting sales taxes from the bulk of their customers. And many of the big Web sellers also voluntarily collect sales taxes in the states that have them. (If you live in Alaska, Delaware, Montana, New Hampshire, or Oregon, you don't pay sales taxes anyway, of course.) But small Internet-only companies generally don't charge sales tax anywhere except their home state. This may change, but for now you can avoid sales taxes on nearly anything you buy simply by ordering it online (or by phone). In some cases you can even walk into a store—say, a shop in the diamond district in New York City—place an order, have it mailed to your home in another state, and avoid sales tax.

Of course, you're supposed to keep track of all of your Internet and interstate purchases and pay the sales tax on them with your state income taxes. But tax experts say that there's no way for states to actually track your purchases or know how much you owe.

A VACATION HOME

You dream of traveling to a place like Paris, Buenos Aires, or San Francisco. And here's the thing: There are people in those cities planning trips, too, some of them maybe even to the place you live, especially if you live in a "destination" spot. So why not simply trade homes with someone for a week? That way nobody has to pay for a hotel or vacation rental. All you need to do is connect with the right people in the place where you want to go—and that's easy, thanks to the Web.

There are a bunch of home-swapping Web sites where you can post an advertisement for your home, including photos and descriptions of the vacation-worthiness of the spot—and where you can peruse the ads posted by people in your favorite locales. Some of these sites charge an annual membership fee, but that's a small price to pay for all the money you'll save on your trip. Fees also help to ensure that everyone posting on the site is serious about swapping.

Swapping your house or apartment means, of course, that strangers will be sleeping in your bed and eating out of your favorite cereal bowl, and so you'll want to be careful to check out the people before turning over your keys. On the other hand, they're opening up their home to you, so there's mutual trust involved. It may help to arrange to meet in person at one location or the other to trade keys and get to know each other a little bit. You can also arrange to have friends stop by to check on things while you're away. (Another alternative is a hospitality exchange, which means you stay at home and act as the other people's hosts, and then they do the same for you in their home.)

To find out more about house swapping (and hospitality exchanges), see who's offering what, or post your own ad, go to:

- *www.couchsurfing.com*
- *www.homeexchange.com*
- *www.craigslist.org*
- *www.home-swap.com*
- *www.digsville.com*
- *www.intervacus.com*
- *www.geenee.com*
- *www.thevacationexchange.com*
- *www.homelink.org*

How to Get Discounts You Aren't Supposed to Know About

Online retailers regularly offer select customers special discounts and freebies. Sometimes these deals are used to reward the company's best customers, or to lure back customers who haven't shopped at the site in many months, or to compensate folks who've had service problems. No matter: *You* can reap the rewards.

That's because these deals are typically administered via coupon codes—combinations of letters and numbers that the customer enters on the checkout page in order to receive the discount. But once the company hands out those codes to some customers, word spreads quickly. In most cases anyone who learns about a code can use it for their own transactions. A host of Web sites specialize in listing the various coupon codes for major online sellers, including www.couponhut.com, www.monkeybargains.com, www.savester.com, www.mybargainbuddy.com, and www.101coolsavings.com. Or just Google the company you'd like a coupon for and add the words "coupon code" (for example, "Enterprise Rent-A-Car coupon code") to get listings.

BARGAIN HUNTING

SPOTTING A DISCOUNT THAT'S DEEP

Megamarts, grocery stores, and pharmacies routinely put products on special so that they can advertise the sale price and draw customers into the store. But just how good a deal is that sale price? Well, there's one way to know when a store is selling something at truly rock bottom: If there's a limit on how many of the sale item each customer can purchase, it means the store is taking a big loss on the discount and doesn't want to lose too much money to any one customer.

Comparing Prices

It's easy to comb the Web for the best price available on almost any new product you're going to buy, especially electronic gadgets. Just log on to a few comparison-shopping sites—such as www.shopzilla.com, www.nextag.com, www.pricegrabber .com, http://shopping.yahoo.com, www.bizrate.com, and www.cnet.com—plug in the product details, and you'll see the prices from a sampling of different e-tailers. Make sure to enter your zip code so that the site can calculate the price including tax (if the store charges tax in your state) and exact shipping costs (if the store charges shipping). Hit a few of these comparison-shopping sites, because they tend to be affiliated with different e-tailers, and you'll know the best possible price for the product. Some comparison sites also offer customer ratings of the sellers, but you can simply take the best price you find (after tax and shipping), call your preferred retailers, and ask them to match it. Also, don't plan a vacation without visiting www.sidestep.com, www.kayak.com, and www.mobissimo.com, which automatically scan hundreds of Web sites for the best prices on hotel rooms, airfare, and other travel arrangements.

Share Your Bulk

Just because your house or apartment is short on storage space doesn't mean that you can't take advantage of the benefits of buying in bulk at warehouse clubs, such as Costco, BJ's, and Sam's, or from online wholesalers. You can join forces with a few friends and share that ninety-six-roll case of toilet paper and eighteen-box package of ziti. All you need is one membership. Shop together so you can agree on what to buy, at least in the beginning, and then split the goods and the tab when you're done.

Brick-and-Mortar Bargains

You certainly don't need to shop online or to hit the megamarts to get bargains. There are deals to be found at plenty of small stores, too, from the national chains to mom-and-pop shops. Here's what to look for:

- As-is products. Many stores offer damaged goods at a steep discount. You might get a box of cereal with a smashed corner for a buck, for instance, even though the Cheerios inside are unharmed. And you can get furniture with a scratch or dent on one side for a fraction of its normal price; just arrange your room so you don't see the damage.

- Floor models. Any store that has a showroom—from the car dealer to the furniture shop to the electronics warehouse—occasionally needs to unload some items that have been on display. Numerous people have tested the product and the original box may be long gone, but you're getting a nearly new product at a discount, and the warranty usually still applies from the date of your purchase (though you should ask about this).

- Going-out-of-business sales. Buying items such as brand-name clothing or kitchen utensils from a store that's closing up shop can be a great way to get a steal on something you normally wouldn't be able to afford. Remember, the nearer the store gets to its final closing day, the deeper the price cuts get—and the emptier the shelves get, too.

> **THE CATCH** Think twice before you buy expensive electronics from a no-name store that's going out of business because you'll have no recourse if you find out the product is faulty. Also, don't assume that the products being sold are the store's original merchandise, because extra products are often brought in by third-party liquidation companies.

- Comparison-pricing Web sites. These aren't just for online shopping anymore. At http://froogle.google.com and www.shoplocal.com, you can enter your zip code and the specific details of the product you're buying; you'll get back a list of stores near you as well as their prices for the object you're seeking.

- Price matching. Online retailers and megamarts typically have lower prices than independent stores because they sell such a high volume, and need to make only a small profit on each item. They often get better wholesale pricing from their suppliers as well. Nonetheless, many small stores will match megamart and online pricing. You'll have to pay sales tax in most states; on the other hand, you won't have to pay for shipping.

- Pawnshops. If you don't mind heading into a seedy part of town and dealing with a seedy pawnbroker, you can find great deals at these places. The items for sale in a pawnshop were either sold to the pawnbroker or used as collateral for a loan that was not repaid. And undoubtedly a few of the items sold in your average pawnshop were stolen, but that may also be true at eBay and flea markets. To find a pawnshop in your area, see www.uspawnshopdirectory.com.

HOW TO ASK FOR HAND-ME-DOWNS

Got an older sibling who seems to always be replacing perfectly nice furniture with something newer and more expensive? Have a friend who's your size and never seems to wear anything twice? Know a couple who are shacking up and clearly have too much stuff between the two of them to fit in their new home?

Maybe they'll offer you their hand-me-downs—but maybe they won't because they're worried you might feel patronized or belittled, or because they just never thought of it. Here are some ways to open the door, politely. (Choose only one of the following, and try to work it naturally into conversation to avoid being obvious.)

- *Make your own offer to them of something of yours that you know they admire and that you no longer need. (Don't force this: It has to be something that they've genuinely remarked on or obviously need, even if they're unlikely to accept the gift.)*
- *Drop a comment about how much you like something of theirs that you think they may not need anymore a year or two down the line.*
- *Mention something in your house that you've gotten as a hand-me-down from a mutual friend or relative.*

If your tactic fails, just come right out and let them know that if they're planning on getting rid of that couch or the slightly used gray flannel suit, they should keep you in mind. Mention it once and leave the rest to them.

EBAY KNOW-HOW

You can find almost anything you want on www.eBay.com—and to a lesser extent at other online auction sites, such as http://auctions.yahoo.com and http://auctions.amazon.com. Just log on to the Web site, type in the keyword for what you want, and you'll see a list of auctions currently under way for that item. If you don't find what you're looking for, check back soon—people are constantly adding new items to the mix. And once you've made a few purchases and understand the system, auction sites are also a great way to turn your unwanted stuff into cash. Here a few tips on buying and selling.

Buying

- Create a PayPal account that's linked to your checking account. PayPal is the service that eBay uses to transfer funds from the buyer to the seller. You give PayPal the money when you place an order or win an auction, and it gets passed along to the seller. That way you're not sharing your personal credit card or bank information with the seller—and if you never get what you paid for, PayPal will generally give you back your money. You can fund your PayPal account with a credit card, but only businesses can accept such transactions, so if the seller is an individual, you need a checking-account-linked PayPal account.

- Before you bid on a product, watch a few auctions for similar items and see what price they wind up selling for. That'll give you a sense of the going rate for that item (of course, the condition and age of the item will affect price, too). Once you have a bead on pricing, you can try to get your item for less than the market rate.

- Never place a bid until the closing moments of an auction. (Most auctions last for a week, and bidding early only drives up the price.) Make your move in the final minute or two of an auction, though, and there's little time for someone else to outbid you.

Selling

- Include a photo of any item you're trying to sell or people just won't bite. You'll get the best results by laying the item on a neutral-colored sheet. Use natural light instead of a flash to minimize shadows and a digital camera to make uploading easy.

- Remember that as the seller, you're the one who pays eBay's cut. You'll pay a small amount (under $5) to list an item; if it sells, you'll pay a portion of the selling price (3 percent for items selling between $25 and $1,000).

- Don't waste your money on packing materials when you need to ship fragile items. Shredded mail, magazines, and catalogs make excellent box filler.

HOW TO BE A SQUEAKY WHEEL

Whether you've been wronged by an error on your credit card statement, are disappointed in a product that you've purchased, or want to complain about bad service you've received, calling the 800 number for customer service can feel like beating your head against the wall. First you have to negotiate an incomprehensible maze of "Press 1 for this" and "Press 2 for that," then you have to wait on hold, and when you finally get to talk to someone, she turns out to be rude and unhelpful. But don't be discouraged. There are waived fees, discount coupons, and free samples at the end of these calls if you play them right:

- Know your adversary. Working as a customer service representative is a low-paying, dead-end job. Reps often work for third-party call centers—in cubbies with thousands of other reps around them—and have no real knowledge about the companies they're providing service for. They're most likely to be in rural America or, increasingly, in India. And the working

■ GET IT FOR FREE

THE SECURITY OF A WATCHDOG

Worried about break-ins, but don't want to invest in an alarm system or a German shepherd? Go for the next best thing: a sign in the window. You can pick up a beware of dog sign at a local hardware store, and you can get alarm company signs at such online sites as www.needdecals.com.

conditions are so poor that employee turnover is about 25 percent per month.

- Be civil. If you yell or swear, you're going on perma-hold, getting disconnected, or getting transferred to the wrong department. So be amicable and always treat the rep as your ally in the solution, not as the cause of the problem.

- Be firm. Even as you're being friendly, make it clear that the problem needs to be resolved one way or another.

- Be brief. Reps get bonuses and raises based on how quickly they can process their calls, so get right to the point without the long-winded sob story. (A simple "My boss/husband/wife is going to kill me for this" is a good quick option.)

- Escalate. The first tier of representative that you speak with has no real power, in many cases. So if he says, "I'm sorry, I cannot do that," ask nicely to speak with someone who can. (This is better than asking for his "supervisor," which implies that you want to complain about him, and is likely to get you put on hold or routed to another rep who's only pretending to be a supervisor.)

- Try Again. If you get an agent with a terrible attitude, just cut your losses and try dialing into the phone center again. Don't hang up on the first representative, though, because that will get noted in your file and could lead the next agent to be cranky, too. Instead, make a pretext like "my baby just woke up early from her nap," or "my boss is coming," and excuse yourself from the conversation.

- Follow up. If you don't get satisfaction from your call, follow up with a letter to someone high up in the company, such as the CEO. Document the original problem and the failure of customer service to resolve it. The CEO won't actually read your letter, of course, but his secretary will, and she knows how to get things done, like rebates, coupons, and other customer appreciation freebies.

{ STYLE CENTS: }
BUDGET DECORATING,
FROM THE THRIFT STORE
TO THE MEGAMART

Keeping up with the Joneses was a
full-time job with my mother and
father. It was not until many years
later when I lived alone that I
realized how much cheaper it was to
drag the Joneses down to my level.

—*Quentin Crisp*

You don't need bags of money to furnish a comfortable and attractive home.
You just need to trust your instincts—and to follow a few basic guidelines.

GREAT DISCOUNT DECORATING

Keep It Simple

When it comes to discount furniture, the less complicated, the better. Simple lines
and materials make no pretense of being ornate or antique, so they don't feel like
fakes. Plus the makers don't waste their limited manufacturing budgets on fan-
cying them up, so they tend to wear better than complicated items. You'll typically
find the simplest designs in modernist, retro, and Shaker styles.

Choose Durable Fabrics

One place where you don't want to skimp is on the quality of upholstery fabrics—
cheap cloth doesn't stand up well to everyday use. Natural materials, such as
leather, cotton, and wool, are generally far superior to synthetics like polyester and
nylon. One durable synthetic alternative, however, is microfiber, which is fabric
woven from synthetic strands that are 1,000 times thinner than a human hair. That
makes the cloth very dense, almost suedelike, thereby reducing the risk of
staining or tearing.

Hunt

To give your home personality, look for unique and interesting items that you can mix in with the commonplace stuff you can get at Target, IKEA, and other megamarts. Browse tag sales, flea markets, swap meets, and eBay—as well as Web sites such as www.craigslist.org and www.freecycle.org—for quirky furniture, art, and accessories. Lamps are great choices for buying secondhand because it's easy to alter their style simply by swapping out the shade; you can buy kits to completely rewire them if there's an electrical problem. Wooden furniture is a safer bet than upholstered goods because the old foam inside upholstery will likely be worn out and uncomfortable—and it can contain mold and mildew if it was ever stored in a basement or left out in the rain. A great way to gauge the fair price for recycled products is by searching completed eBay auctions for similar items. Remember, too, that you're likely to get a better tag-sale deal in the late afternoon than the early morning. That's when people are most eager to unload their remaining stuff.

Pick What You Like

Don't worry about matching the architectural style of your home, about having matching furniture sets, or about whether something is fashionable or not. Just select things that appeal to you and that feel right for your lifestyle, your home, and one another. The trick is to find some echo that makes the components of the space feel right together. It can be texture, shape, style, origin, or just the overall sensibility of the items. And you can always create the connection by painting disparate things—such as mismatched dining room chairs, bookshelves, or end tables—in a single color scheme, or by reupholstering mismatched overstuffed furniture in a single fabric.

Reuse and Recycle

Look for unusual ways to solve decorating problems and you'll not only create a one-of-a-kind look but save money as well. There's no end to the possibilities, but here are a few suggestions made from items you can find for free or purchase cheap at flea markets, tag sales, and architectural salvage yards:

ORIGINAL ITEM	NEW USE
Old panel door	Cut to size, bolt on legs, and set into place as headboard.
Shutters	Use hinges to fasten three large shutters together as a screen.
Metal plant stand	Load with clean towels or toilet paper in a guest bathroom.
Beach rocks	Glue onto dresser drawer knobs.
Plastic PVC plumbing pipe	Paint and use as a stairway handrail.
Classic toy dump truck	Use as a houseplant container.
Antique ladder	Set against a bathroom wall for use as a towel rack.
1950s hand towels	Sew together for table runners or curtains.
Quirky serving trays	Hang as wall art.
Coffee cans	Cover with wrapping paper and use as desk organizers.
Wooden crates	Paint and hang on the wall as curio cabinets.
Ceramic tiles	Put felt dots on the bottom and use them as wall hangings, coasters, and hot plates.
Antique glass bottles	Add pour spouts and use them as decanters for kitchen and bath soaps and moisturizers.
Giant cable spools	Stand them on end and cover with fabric to make end tables or nightstands.

Look for the Beauty in Functional Things

Many utilitarian household items are intrinsically beautiful. If you store them out in the open, they can do double duty as decoration. For example, put your dry pantry goods in snap-top glass canisters and display their colorful contents—from red beans to blue cornmeal, yellow pasta to brown sugar—on an open kitchen shelf. Other attractive items that might be worthy of exposed storage include bathroom towels, pots and pans, hot sauces, dried spices, kitchen utensils, fireplace logs, serving platters, and cookbooks.

Avoid Clutter

All homes that feel comfortable and look good share one thing: an uncluttered, relaxed atmosphere. Give your furniture, artwork, accessories—and guests—some elbow room. That means open spaces, and it means not using a lot of busy patterns together. Choose a focal point or two for the room, and let everything else be understated.

TAKE YOUR TIME

If you can be patient about decorating your home, you can save a lot of money:

- *You can wait to purchase big-ticket items until they go on sale.*

- *The more time you wait, the greater your chance of finding a hand-me-down or a Craigslist score before you shell out full retail for a product.*

- *You'll learn the way you really live in the house and what it really needs, so you don't wind up making impulsive decorating decisions that you need to redo later.*

- *You can stage your purchases over the long term, which will make it far easier to fit everything you need in your budget.*

BARGAIN HUNTING

■ BARGAIN HUNTING

GOVERNMENT SURPLUS

The army-navy surplus store has gone virtual. You can now log on to www.gsaauctions.gov to view and bid on products ranging from furniture to household appliances to office equipment (as well as cars, trucks, and even airplanes!).

■

THINK LIKE A PROFESSIONAL DECORATOR

Interior decorators pride themselves on their senses of style, their Rolodexes full of great sources, and their eyes for color, but much of what they do comes down to some basic principles of design that anyone can follow:

- As a rule, dark colors tend to make spaces feel smaller while light ones make them feel larger. So choosing a light color for the walls can lend a sense of space to a compact room. And painting the ceiling white can help make it feel higher. Busy prints on fabrics and wallpapers, as well as complex grids of small tiles, work like dark colors and make spaces feel smaller.

- Horizontal lines tend to make a surface—a wall, a floor, or whatever—seem wider, while vertical lines make it feel longer. Diagonal lines make surfaces seem more dramatic and larger.

- Neutral colors—white, beige, tan, as well as natural wood and stone—never go out of style and so don't run the risk of turning off potential buyers when it's time to sell your house. That's why it's a good idea to choose them for permanent elements of the space, such as tiles, countertops, and cabinetry. Then let the bold colors come from the accents, which are easy to change when you tire of them or when someone else buys the house.

- Every well-designed room needs a focal point, which means a centerpiece that commands the lion's share of attention in the space. It might be a fireplace in the living room, a picture window in the dining room, a professional-style kitchen range in the kitchen, or a claw-foot tub in the bathroom. For spaces that don't have obvious focal points, think about adding a large piece of furniture or artwork that can serve the purpose.

- Try to break up big expanses of a single color with something contrasting—such as red throw pillows on a solid green sofa, or a brown armoire in the midst of a cream wall.

- Think about your decor like you think about your wardrobe: Choose items that fit your sense of style and combine well with the ensemble in the room—and let the accessories do the heavy lifting. Bold and colorful accent pieces cost a lot less than stunningly beautiful pieces of furniture, so keep the big-ticket items simple and let the pizzazz come from wall hangings, trinkets, throw pillows, and other details.

FURNISHINGS ON THE CHEAP

Ah, the joys of a new home. It feels so open and spacious—especially since you don't have enough furniture to fill it! Here's how to furnish a home without sinking yourself into credit card debt.

Hit the Road, Save 40 to 70 Percent

Sixty percent of all furniture that's manufactured in the United States comes from the area around two towns in North Carolina, High Point and Hickory. And so, depending on where you live, when you're ready to make a large furniture purchase, it might just be worth the effort to rent a U-Haul and take a road trip to shop at the manufacturers' outlet stores, where the discounts range from 40 percent for custom orders to 70 percent for stock items. You'll need to plan ahead, of course, and for that you'll want to hit the local library or Amazon.com for *Shopping the North Carolina Furniture Outlets* by Ellen R. Shapiro (Three Rivers Press, 2003), which will teach you where to go for the best deals on different kinds of furniture—and the best-tasting Tar Heel barbecue. You can also go on the Web and check out www.highpoint.org for more information on furniture shops in the Highpoint area.

IKEA—Hurts So Good

If you've never been to an IKEA, you're missing out on a revolution in home design. This Scandinavian company has transformed the market for well-designed, great-looking home furnishings by offering striking minimalist wood, steel, and plastic products at dirt-cheap prices. But be forewarned: IKEA is not a run-of-the-mill retailer. It's a totally do-it-yourself shopping experience. You'll have to find what you want on the display floor, then locate it yourself in the massive warehouse, and then assemble it yourself at home later. Be sure to check out the "hurts room" where items with minor damage are sold for even less—and remember that some IKEA stores also rent trucks to make it easier to get your loot home.

THE CATCH

IKEA sells a la carte. Don't assume you've got everything you need in the package, because items such as mounting hardware aren't always included.

Unfinished Business

If you're handy with a paintbrush, unfinished furniture is one of the least expensive ways to get solid wood pieces for your home. Look for an unfinished-furniture shop near you, or order online from Gothic Cabinet Craft (888–801–3100, www .gothiccabinetcraft.com). In either case, you aren't always limited to the selection you see. Most shops will custom-size their cabinets, tables, shelves, and chairs to order. They'll even paint or stain them for you in your choice of finish—though you'll save money by doing that job yourself.

Knocked Down, but Not Out

An ever-growing percentage of the affordable furniture market consists of "knock-down" products—pieces that arrive packed flat in a box for the consumer to assemble. Makers see big savings from these ready-to-assemble kits because they take up far less room on shipping trucks and retail shelves than do full-size furniture pieces. Yet producing furniture this way generally doesn't detract from the quality of the product. So knock-down furniture and cabinetry can provide decent quality at a discount price, and they're right there on the megamart shelf for you to take home that day, rather than waiting many weeks for delivery of a pre-assembled product.

THE CATCH

You'll need to set aside an unrushed and uninterrupted afternoon to put your new furniture together. }

(OR RIDICULOUSLY CHEAP)

GET IT FOR FREE

PROFESSIONAL HELP

It's easy to be skeptical of the advice you get from salespeople since they have a vested interest in selling their products, but many retailers actually offer free design help that's well worth the asking. Furniture stores have in-house interior decorators, home centers have kitchen and bath designers, paint stores have trained decorating experts, and hardware stores have knowledgeable handy-men, all of whom dole out free advice to serious customers—often before you whip out your charge card.

THE CATCH

Like salespeople, designers often get paid on commission for what they sell, so keep in mind that they're likely to push for the more expensive option. }

EVEN CHEAPER FURNITURE STRATEGIES: THE FOUR Rs

Used furniture—especially stuff built before World War II—is often better constructed than what's manufactured these days. With a little ingenuity and some touching up, you can score a real find for much less than what you'd pay for new. Heck, come bulk trash day, you might even get it for free!

Rescue It: Dumpster Diving

Warning: This is for die-hard Cheap Bastards only. If you're squeamish about poking through other people's garbage or sniffing street finds for unpleasant scents, this hunt is not for you. But if you're willing to get down and dirty for a few hours in exchange for some great freebie finds, searching the streets for other people's castaways can yield just about whatever you're looking for. Here are some critical tips:

- Pick your moment. The turn of the month—that is, the last day of one month and the first day of the next—is the time to go on your hunt, because that's when people move—and when people move, they get rid of good stuff they don't want to haul.

- Bring a (good) friend. This is a two-person job, because you need to do some heavy lifting. It works best when both people are hoping to find things to take home—preferably different kinds of things.

- Head uptown. Not surprisingly, the stuff that gets thrown away in well-heeled neighborhoods is of a higher quality than the stuff that gets thrown away in the cheap-rent districts.

DON'T WASTE YOUR MONEY ON

■ DON'T WASTE YOUR MONEY ON

. . . RENT-TO-OWN FURNISHINGS.

You'll wind up paying a lot more for that big-screen television or living room set by renting it than buying it. Plus, in some cases you won't be able to cancel the arrangement early thanks to fine print in the contract. You're far better off taking a loan, buying on layaway, or simply sticking with purchases you can really afford!

- Dress appropriately. No matter how hot it is, wear long pants and sleeves, steel-toed boots, leather gloves, and a hat.

- Know your needs. You may, of course, come across some unexpected find that you can't pass up, but it's a good idea to set out with some goals for the things you need—including their sizes. In other words, measure the space you have for the desk, armchair, or kitchen table you want, jot down the sizes, and bring along both your notes and a measuring tape.

- Plan for transportation. Whether you'll be using a rented pickup truck, the roof rack on your aging Subaru Outback, or a hand-powered dolly, have your wheels ready and waiting. Trying to work out the transportation after making a find leads to frustration, lost time, and the chance that someone else will grab your new sofa when you leave it alone for a few minutes.

- Remember the hot-shower-and-cold-beer rule. Once you've scoured the streets and Dumpsters and brought home your finds, it's time for a very hot shower—and then a few very cold drinks. (The person who scored the best loot should buy.)

Repair It

When antiques dealers search tag sales for great finds, they ignore the inevitable minor blemishes on the furniture because they know they'll repair the problems before sticking them in the shop window. Here are some simple tricks for your own furniture restoration jobs:

- Water marks, which often look like white rings, occur when moisture works into the finish. To remove them, place a few sheets of paper towel over them and then press down with a warm iron.

- Fill scratches with a child's crayon in the closest possible color.

- Remove gum by holding an ice cube over it and then scraping it away with an expired credit card.

- Get rid of paint drips, sticker residue, and other stuck-on gunk using Goof Off, a product sold at paint supply stores.

- Reattach loose components by painting wood glue on each end, pressing them together, and clamping for twenty-four hours with quick-grip clamps or wrapping them tightly with string and tying it off like a tourniquet.

- Resolve stained upholstery—and bad fabric choices—with slipcovers, which you can make yourself or purchase in standard sizes at home decorating stores.

- Loosen sticky drawers by treating the areas where wood meets wood using linseed oil or carnauba wax, either of which you can pick up at a hardware store.

- Restore faded mirrors by bringing them to a glass shop to have a fresh coat of silver painted on the back. Not all glass shops offer this service, however, so call ahead.

- Removing cigarette burns is a big job, so if possible, simply place a table topper over the surface to hide them. To remove them you'll need to sand out the blemish and refinish the piece—or fill in the indentation with putty and then paint the piece.

Refinish It

Refinishing means stripping the old paint or varnish from the wood, then applying stain and polyurethane. It's a messy job that requires harsh chemicals and plenty of elbow grease—and it should be done outside to make sure you're getting plenty of fresh air. Most chemical strippers are very nasty to work with, but there is a safe and effective product that you can use: Back to Nature Multi-Strip (www.ibacktonature.com). Then you can apply stain if you want to darken the wood, plus a few coats of polyurethane to protect the surface. Your local library almost surely has a few instruction books about refinishing. If not, ask them to order *Weekend Refinisher* (Ballantine).

Reupholster It

This final R involves stretching foam and fabric tightly over the frame of your furniture piece and then fastening it in place with staples or tacks. It's a good idea to practice your technique on a few items that you don't care much about before tackling something special. Again, there should be some books at your library that offer good step-by-step instructions, such as *Simply Upholstery* (Sunset) or *Upholstery Basics* (Creative Publishing International).

BOLD IS BEAUTIFUL— AND PAINT IS CHEAP

Nothing affects the feel of a space as much as putting some color on the walls. And since cans of paint don't cost much, even buying a different color for every room doesn't require a large investment. (You can avoid having to buy too many different paints by using a single ceiling white throughout the house, and perhaps a single cream for the trimwork, too.) So forget white-on-white and give your home some bold colors. You can choose any palette you like, but there are a few tried-and-true tricks for ensuring good color combinations.

Understanding the basics of how to choose color starts with remembering your preschool lessons about primary colors, which are the three colors that can't be created by mixing others: red, blue, and yellow. Imagine spacing them evenly on a wheel. Then, between them, put the color created by mixing the two adjacent colors. So between red and blue goes purple, between blue and yellow goes green, and between yellow and red goes orange. Add two more rounds of mixed colors and you have the color wheel. Now you can use this imaginary wheel to create a host of different color schemes:

- Monochrome. As the name suggests, this approach uses either a single color or a mix of colors that are very close on the wheel. Visual interest can be provided by contrasts in textures or by a few furnishings in contrasting colors.

- Analogous. Colors that are near each other on the color wheel—such as blues and greens—are analogous colors, and two or three analogous colors can create a rich color scheme. Usually one color dominates; the other two are used more sparingly.

- Complementary. Another approach is to use colors that sit directly opposite each other on the color wheel, such as red and green. These contrasting colors can create an eye-catching color scheme. Generally one is used as the main color in the room while the other is used as an accent.

To see an example of a color wheel, visit www.colormatters.com; click on "Design & Art," then "Color Theory." For more information about choosing paint combinations, check out the interactive paint selection tools offered by various paint manufacturers, including those at www.benjaminmoore.com and www.sherwin-williams.com.

FINISHING TOUCHES

Your home will never look fully lived in and cozy until you have art on the walls and knickknacks on the shelves. And, just as with gifts, the best ones are the ones you make yourself (for practically nothing).

Creative Accents

If you let your imagination shine through, you can create your own decorative details, such as:

- Black-and-white photographs. Got an eye for photography? Turn it to good use the next time you're traveling, even just on a walk around the neighborhood. Use black-and-white film—or the black-and-white setting on your digital camera—and shoot interesting trees and flowers (think Ansel Adams), landscapes (especially if you're passing through Big Sky country on a road trip), or Americana (things like diners, street musicians, and quirky houses make great subjects). Have the best images printed in a large format, such as 16 by 20 inches, load them into store-bought frames, and you've got great one-of-a-kind artwork.

- Beach and hike finds. Natural objects such as shells, rocks, pinecones, leaves, and beach glass can be used as beautiful decorations, especially for bathrooms in the case of objects found at the beach.

- Painted effects. Bring texture to the walls by sponge-painting them—a simple procedure in which you use a sponge to apply a coat of paint over a previous coat that's in a lighter shade. Or create vertical or horizontal stripes of color by doing some careful measuring and masking off with blue painter's tape before applying the different paints.

- Interesting fabrics and papers. Any colorful and interesting fabric can become a wall hanging, from that handwoven blanket you bought for ten pesos on a Mexican beach to that hand-me-down quilt your grandmother made. And leftover bits of wallpaper or wrapping paper can be placed into do-it-yourself frames and hung as art—or use them to wrap lamp shades or wastepaper baskets.

- Dried plants and flowers. It's easy to dry flowers, foliage, and berries for use in homemade wreaths, boughs, and arrangements that will last forever. You can hang them upside down in a cool, well-ventilated, and dark space, or use a drying agent sold at craft supply stores.

Collecting

People with tons of money like to collect objects such as furniture made by the famous Eames brothers, original lithographs by the nineteenth-century bird-watcher John James Audubon, or Beatles memorabilia. But there are a lot of inexpensive things that make for interesting collections, too. You could collect colorful 1950s neon signs, snow globes from around the world, antique woodworking tools, early radios, fruit crate labels, vintage Pez dispensers, or whatever else interests you. Scour yard sales, junk shops, and eBay to find the items, then put them on display to bring unique personality to your home.

If the items are fragile or valuable, you'll want to keep them out of harm's way by grouping them behind the glass doors of a china or curio cabinet. Or make your own protective case by using hinges to fasten an old sash window to the face of a size-matched bookshelf. Another option is to place the objects on a high shelf that's above arm's reach, assuming the collection can be seen and appreciated at that height. If the objects are durable enough for regular handling, though, you don't need to put them behind glass. You can simply arrange them on a shelf, windowsill, mantel, or tabletop.

Budget-Friendly Faux?

Things aren't always what they seem. Sometimes they're much cheaper materials masquerading as upscale products. Here are some of the best "faux" products on the market. All are practically indistinguishable from the real thing and will save you major dough. (*Note:* There are many brands to choose from; the Web sites listed here are just to give you an idea of what's available.)

- Porcelain tiles that look like granite, slate, limestone, or other natural stones cost far less than the real thing, and they're more water and scratch resistant, too. (http://daltileproducts.com)

- Lightweight foam planting containers that look like metal, stone, or cast concrete make these looks attainable—in terms of both price and the ability to cart them home. (www.gardeners.com)

- Cabinets, paneling, and doors that look like stained wood but are actually made from fiberboard with images of wood grain on their surfaces not only save you money but are also less prone to warping and cracking than real wood. (www.cabinetmart.com)

- Snap-together floors that look like wood or tile but are actually photographs under a sheet of plastic can cost just a quarter of the price of the real thing—and they're a cinch to install yourself. (www.pergo.com)

- Manufactured countertops made with stone dust have the look of slab stone for a slightly cheaper price. They're also far more durable than most types of stone and can be molded into any configuration, often without any seams. (www.caesarstoneus.com)

- Synthetic stones that look like fieldstone walls or chimneys but are actually human-made veneers cost far less than real stone, especially since they can be installed by a tiling contractor instead of a much pricier mason. (www.culturedstoneus.com)

- Roofing shingles that look like slate but are made from recycled rubber offer a less expensive and lighter-weight alternative for old slate roofs that need replacement. (http://ecostarinc.com)

- Plastic trim boards that get cut, nailed, and painted just like wood cost less than high-grade exterior-grade wood, and they also won't warp or rot, so you'll save a bundle on long-term maintenance. (www.azek.com)

- Shingles and clapboards made from fiber cement cost more than wood initially, but they won't rot and never need painting, so they cost less over the long haul. (http://jameshardie.com)

BARGAIN HUNTING

MAIL-ORDER LAMPS

Two mail-order companies sell an amazing selection of lamps and light fixtures at seriously marked-down prices: www.lampsplus.com and www.lampsusa.com. Even if you prefer to see the lamps in person before you buy, it's worth a visit to these sites so that you can ask your local store to match their prices.

■ WORTH THE MONEY

WORTH THE MONEY

PAINT-BY-NUMBERS KITS

Here's a great way to turn photographs into pop art. E-mail your pictures to the folks at Koko's (www.paintbynumberkit.com), and you'll get back a canvas with a color-coded pattern printed on it, along with a matching set of acrylic paints and brushes for coloring it in. Follow the company's recommendations for what kind of photo to use. The results are well worth the cost: Kits start at under $50.

■

Bargain Art

Forget about the clichés at the home center; you can choose any art you want for your walls by shopping online:

Art.com (800–952–5592)

From high-quality reproductions of museum paintings to limited-edition prints by unknown artists, you can get it here for cheap. You can even have your own photographs electronically transformed into what looks like an impressionist painting.

AllPosters.com (888–654–0143)

Whether your taste runs more toward Einstein with his tongue sticking out, vintage champagne advertisements in French, landscape photography, or virtually any other type of poster, this is the place to find it. There are more than 300,000 available, categorized by artist, subject, and theme. Select the frame and matting that you want and it'll arrive at your door ready to hang—at a fraction of the cost that a brick-and-mortar frame shop would charge.

1–800–posters.com

This is the place to shop for what you might call dorm decor. Categories include cheesecake, beefcake, cannabis, music, movies, vehicles, sports—and the site has various takes on dogs playing poker, too.

OverstockArt.com (866–686–1888)

Why get a poster of your favorite Picasso or Monet when you can have the painting for less than $100? Okay, these aren't the real thing, of course, but they are kind of fun. Instead of being printed on paper, these reproductions have been rendered with real oil paints on canvas, so you get the texture of an original artwork. All in all, they offer a quirky way to bring classic art into your home. Make a game of trying to convince your most gullible guests that you actually own Edvard Munch's *The Scream.*

HOW TO GET ON A TV MAKEOVER SHOW

There are now dozens of reality TV shows dedicated to home improvement, from Curb Appeal *to* While You Were Out, Trading Spaces *to* Extreme Home Makeover. *And the fuel that drives them all is real people with real houses, so you'd think it would be easy to get on the air and get the free gear and free expertise that's often part of the bargain. But for every household that makes it onto television, about 2,000 apply.*

More than anything, producers want attractive people with outgoing personalities and some colorful story to tell. So the best way to boost your odds of success is to send in a video in which you show off your space— and yourself. Have fun, be creative, and try to find an interesting reason that the show should choose you. If you have a collection of rare musical instruments from around the world, you live with five coed roommates, or your home is an antique RV, your pitch will have a lot more appeal than the approach that most people take, which is to say, "I want to be on your show because my house really needs work and I want a free makeover."

To find out how to apply, just watch the shows, many of which announce when they're searching for participants and how to apply at the end of their episodes. Or you can log on to the cable networks' Web sites for more information:

- *www.hgtv.com/hgtv*
- *www.diynetwork.com/diy*
- *www.tlc.discovery.com/fansites/apply/getontlc.html?*

Making Cut Flowers Last

Whether you cut them from your own garden or purchase them from a florist, fresh flowers are great decorating tools, bringing bright colors, wonderful scents, and life to your home. Here's how to keep them fresh for as long as possible:

1. Use a sharp knife or shears to cut the end off the stems before placing them in the vase. Angling the knife at forty-five degrees will reduce the chances of crushing the stem and prevent the cut end from sitting flat on the bottom of the vase, which would prevent the uptake of water.

2. Remove all thorns and leaves that will sit below the waterline.

3. Fill the vase with warm water, which is better absorbed by the flowers than cold. Also, add the preservative packet provided by the florist—or make your own preservative by mixing 2 tablespoons white vinegar, 2 tablespoons sugar, ½ teaspoon household chlorine bleach, and 1 quart water. (It's a fallacy that placing a crushed aspirin or a penny in the vase will extend the flowers' lives.)

4. Place the vase far from sunshine, heating vents, and the path of fans, all of which hasten decay.

5. Move the arrangement into the refrigerator or a cool cellar overnight. This can double the life of your bouquet, as long as the flowers never get any colder than thirty-five degrees.

6. Recut the stems every few days to expose fresh ends, and keep topping off the water.

7. When the first flowers begin to wither and turn brown, remove them, but if other flowers still look good, leave them in the vase.

Scents and Sounds

The vast majority of decorating addresses the sense of sight—and to a lesser extent touch, in the case of upholstery fabrics, pillowcases, and the like. But two other senses have a big impact on life in our homes: It's important to plan for good sounds and scents, too.

Whether it's the Chinese take-out place downstairs, a musty basement, or just the everyday smells of a busy household, the air in your home may not always feel fresh. The best way to avoid nuisance smells is to keep your house clean, combat basement moisture with a dehumidifier, and keep some houseplants around to clean the air. Then you can battle problem smells by opening windows now and then—and with aromatic candles if you like.

Noisy neighbors, passing traffic, and fire engines can make quite a racket. Consider a white-noise machine to mask those sounds at night, and a water fountain (see www.kineticfountains.com and www.simplyfountains.com for numerous choices under $50) to provide comforting cover during the day.

ONE YOU NEED

AN INDOOR CITRUS TREE

Dwarf citrus plants offer beautiful foliage, fragrant flowers, and delicious fruit—and you can grow them in practically any climate by treating them as houseplants. Try Meyer lemons, which are sweeter than commercial lemons and easier to grow, or Trovita oranges—easy to grow indoors, and they taste great, too. You can purchase either of these plants for under $35, including shipping, by visiting www.four windsgrowers.com—not a bad deal for something that will add appeal to your home for many years to come.

THE CATCH
Citrus plants need eight to twelve hours of sunlight during flower and fruit season, so if you live in a cold-winter climate, you may need to bring them outside in spring, which is when they produce fruit.

EMPLOYEE DISCOUNTS

Longing for one of those pricey Pottery Barn leather club chairs or Mission-style Restoration Hardware china cabinets? Here's how you can get them at a steep discount: Fill out a job application. Many retailers hire extra help around the holidays, and in exchange for your part-time efforts helping throngs of stressed-out shoppers, you'll get more than a modest hourly pay rate: You'll also qualify for a hefty discount, often 30 to 40 percent off anything in the store—making a high-end splurge a lot more affordable.

SLEEP CHEAP

When it comes to mattresses, always buy new (or take hand-me-downs from people you know), because used mattresses can contain allergens, mold, and all sorts of other unpleasantness. But that doesn't mean you need to shop at department stores or mattress chains where the prices for brand-name mattresses are exorbitant.

Trying to comparison-shop for mattresses makes used-car shopping look simple. No two mattress stores carry the same models—or maybe they do, but the names are different, so how would you know? What's more, the salesclerks share little if any information about how the mattresses were made or what the quality or firmness differences are among them. That leaves you with little to go on, other than brand name, how the bed feels when you lie on it for a few minutes, and the old adage that you get what you pay for (which isn't always true with mattresses).

But there is another way. You can skip the department stores and mainstream mattress shops (such as Sleepy's and 1–800–Mattress) and go to an independent mattress manufacturer. Many of these old-time companies have been put *out of business by the big name brands, but you can still find them in some areas. There's the E. J. Schrader Co. in West Palm Beach, Florida, for example (www.schraderbeds.com); the McCroskey Mattress Company in San Francisco (www.mcroskey.com); the Norwalk Mattress Company in Norwalk, Connecticut (www.norwalkmattress.com); and dozens more across the country. They all sell direct to the consumer, offering good quality at an affordable price. Check the yellow pages for "Mattresses, Manufacturers" to find a company near you.*

DON'T WASTE YOUR MONEY ON

. . . REFINISHING OR COVERING OLD WOOD FLOORS.

If refinishing is not in the budget, you can simply coat the floors with primer and paint designed for the job, and get beautiful and durable results for a tiny cash layout.

{ROOMS FOR IMPROVEMENT: MONEY-SAVING STRATEGIES FOR EVERY PART OF THE HOUSE}

The remarkable thing about my
mother is that for 30 years she served
us nothing but leftovers. The original
meal has never been found.

—Calvin Trillin

Trying to live frugally is like swimming against a riptide. America worships consumption; conservation and thrift are lost arts. Take the "sell-by" date on a carton of eggs: What does that mean? Are they still edible the day after? What about three days later, or a week? And how are you supposed to know how much of a tax write-off you can legitimately take for that pile of worn-out clothing you finally cleaned out of your closet and donated to Goodwill? What can homeowners do to combat steep heating costs—short of just leaving on the down parkas while you're in the house? Well, we're going to answer these and other home economics questions once and for all.

ENTRYWAYS

You don't need a mudroom to have a place to hang wet raincoats, stack outdoor gear, or towel off Fido. All you need are a few simple organizational tools placed by the entry door that you use most—whether it's in a back hall or a corner of the kitchen. You'll want a few key hooks, for example; a small table or shelf where you can stash everything from loose change to mail when you come in the door; and a boot tray, which can be made from a simple tin cookie sheet. If space permits, a coat rack or some coat hooks are handy, too.

Draft Dodgers: Blocking Door Drafts

Heat can pour out of the gaps around an old wood door, especially if it doesn't fit perfectly into its frame anymore. Here are three tools for blocking that heat loss:

1. Weatherstripping. Rubber, foam, or metal strips can be glued or nailed to the doorjamb so that when the door closes, it presses against them and seals the gaps. In conjunction with a door sweep—a fin that gets installed on the bottom edge of the door and rides across the floor to close that gap—weatherstripping typically costs $20 to $30 per door, and is easy to install and effective. Consult your hardware store clerk about which type will be best for your door.

2. A storm door. If your front door is thin, heat may also be migrating right through it. Block its path by installing a storm door, which creates an insulating pocket of air between the doors when they're closed. You can order a storm door through a lumberyard or home center, typically for $100 to $300—an investment that will quickly pay for itself in lowered heating costs. Installation is simple and is fully explained in the enclosed instructions.

3. Draft dogs. Lay one of these snake-shaped beanbags at the base of a door, and it'll block drafts that try to blow underneath. You can get them in a host of kitschy designs (such as dogs, cats, and country plaids) from any number of catalogs. For a more sophisticated solid-color look, check out www.solutionscatalog.com. Or go the really cheap route and make your own draft dog with a rolled-up towel or blanket.

KITCHENS

One place where starter homes and apartments typically leave something to be desired is in the kitchen. Whether you have a compact L-shaped kitchen or nothing more than a galley, the chances are that you don't have enough cabinets or countertops. And unless you're just back from a honeymoon and have boxes full of pots and pans and other gear awaiting you, you're probably in need of some equipment essentials, too. Here's how to make the most of your budget.

Upgrading Kitchen Cabinets

The quickest way to transform an old kitchen is to replace cabinet knobs and pulls. This has a surprisingly transformative effect for such a simple DIY job.

You can also paint dated and dingy cabinets. Just make sure to remove all doors and drawers, take off the hardware, and wash down any stained or greasy surfaces with painter's detergent before you open a can of paint. There are even paints formulated for sticking to the slick surfaces of laminate cabinets.

Another alternative is to reface the old cabinets, which means replacing the doors and drawer fronts, and using a matching material to cover all the exposed faces of the cabinet boxes. The results look so authentic that everyone will think you got new cabinets. For refacing companies, look online, check out the yellow pages, or contact Cabinetpak Kitchens, (800) 323–9510, www.cabinetpak.com; or Kitchen Solvers, (800) 845–6779, www.kitchensolvers.com.

To improve the storage capacity and the convenience of cabinet interiors, check out the slide-out bins, storage racks, door hooks, and other accessories at www.containerstore.com, www.organize.com, and www.stacksandstacks.com.

Wallet-Friendly Kitchen Upgrades

- Countertops. As long as the old countertop isn't waterlogged or cracked, you may be able to install a new surface right over the old thing. Ceramic and stone tiles can often be laid atop stable laminate and tile countertops, as can a new sheet of laminate.

- Floors. The chances are good that underneath that worn-out linoleum, there's a hardwood floor waiting to be exposed. Alternatively, you may be able to install a new vinyl, linoleum, tile, or laminate floor on top of the existing floor. You just need to be careful that you don't build up the floor thickness so much that you permanently trap the dishwasher under the countertop.

THE CATCH Some old floor coverings contain asbestos, so hire a pro to remove the built-up layers, or consult a how-to book about taking proper health precautions. }

- Appliances. Some appliances can be fitted with standard wood or stainless-steel panels to transform their appearance. Another option for high-quality fixtures that just need some sprucing up is to send them to an auto body shop, where they can be repainted.

Organizing Pantries

Whether you're lucky enough to have an actual pantry closet or cabinet, you make do with a few shelves alongside the basement stairs, or you pack everything into a few wall cabinets, here are some ways to organize your ingredients. You can get the products mentioned here at home centers, as well as www.organize.com and www.stacksandstacks.com.

- Maximize shelf space. You can buy accessories that create multiple levels of storage on any given shelf while still maintaining easy access to the goods on the first level. Or you can get stepped inserts that raise up the stuff in the back so you can see it.

- Use glass canisters. Jars with snap-top lids will keep moths and other bugs out of your dry goods, and will make everything from brown sugar to red beans and yellow cornmeal look great when stored in plain sight.

- Install lazy Susans and bin pullouts. These heavy-duty plastic or metal racks make it easy to reach the stuff hiding deep inside base cabinets—especially in those hard-to-reach corner units.

- Organize by theme. If your pantry is a jumble that only you can figure out, it's not organized in the most space-efficient manner. Try putting things into logical groupings, such as baking supplies, coffee gear, breakfast foods, and junk food.

- Line 'em up. Put taller things behind shorter ones, and align duplicates. Try to arrange all shelves so that you can see everything without moving other products—or at least so you know exactly what you need to move to get to it.

THE GROCERY GAME

The Web site www.thegrocerygame.com gives you a list of what's on sale at your local supermarket cross-referenced with the coupons in the newspaper that week, so you can plan your weekly menu based on ingredients you can get for a bargain. The site will also teach you how to stock up on certain items at certain times for the best prices—and it offers links to printable manufacturers' coupons. It costs $10 for an eight-week subscription, although you can get your first four weeks for $1.

Making Sense of Expiration Dates and Sell-By Dates

You cringe at the thought of throwing away food that has gone uneaten, but you're also not a big fan of eating rancid, rotten, or moldy foods. So when should you really toss that unopened jug of yogurt with the week-old sell-by date? Do ground spices ever go bad? Will freezing food make it last virtually forever? Here's the lowdown on exactly how long you can keep your food before you need to either use it up or toss it out, courtesy of the food science program at Kansas State University. Unless otherwise noted, all countdowns begin at either the sell-by date or when the package is opened (and then resealed as tightly as possible), whichever comes first.

THE CATCH
Some aging refrigerators don't keep food at optimal temperatures, and sometimes food goes bad early for no apparent reason. When in doubt, throw it out.

PRODUCT	SHELF LIFE IN CUPBOARD (70 DEGREES)	SHELF LIFE IN FRIDGE (35–40 DEGREES)	SHELF LIFE IN FREEZER (0 DEGREES)
Apples		1–3 weeks from harvest	8–12 months from harvest
Berries		1–2 days from packed-on date	8–12 months from packed-on date
Bread (store-bought)		2–3 weeks	2–3 months
Butter		3 months	12 months
Cookies			
homemade	2–3 weeks (stored in airtight container)		
store-bought	2 months after opening (stored in airtight container)		
Baking mixes (cake, brownie, pancake)	6–9 months		
Canned goods (unopened)	until expiration date or 1 year if there's no date		
Cereal	until expiration date unopened, or 2–3 months from opening (keep inner bag folded shut)		
Cheese			
cottage		5–7 days	1 month (will change texture)
cream		2 weeks	1 month (will change texture)
hard (cheddar/mozzarella)		2–3 months or 2–3 weeks after opening	6–8 months
grated (Parmesan/Romano)		12 months	
Citrus fruits		3 weeks	4–6 months
Condiments (ketchup, mustard)		6–12 months after opening	
Corn			
fresh, in husk		1–2 days from picking	
off the cob, frozen			8–12 months
Eggs			
fresh		2–5 weeks from sell-by date	
hard-boiled		2 weeks from cooking date	
Fish			
white fish fillets		3–5 days from packed-on date	3–6 months from packed-on date
salmon steaks		3–5 days from packed-on date	2 months from packed-on date

PRODUCT	SHELF LIFE IN CUPBOARD (70 DEGREES)	SHELF LIFE IN FRIDGE (35–40 DEGREES)	SHELF LIFE IN FREEZER (0 DEGREES)
Flour	6–8 months		
Fruit juices		until expiration date unopened, or 1 week after opening	12 months
Leftovers		2–4 days from original cooking	2–3 months from original cooking
Lettuce (and other salad greens)		1 week from sell-by date	
Margarine		3 months	12 months
Meat			
beef roasts and steaks		3–5 days from packed-on date	6–12 months from packed-on date
chicken pieces		1–2 days from packed-on date	9 months from packed-on date
ground beef/pork		1–2 days from packed-on date	3–4 months from packed-on date
hot dogs and sausages		2 weeks from sell-by date or 7 days after opening package	1–2 months
turkey pieces		1–2 days from packed-on date	6 months from packed-on date
Melons		1 week	8–12 months
Milk		3–5 days after sell-by date or opening	
Onions	2 weeks		
Pasta and white rice	1–2 years		
Potatoes	2–4 weeks		
Spices (ground)	6 months	6–12 months	12 months
Sugar (granulated)	2 years (in airtight canister)		
Tomatoes (ripe)		5–6 days	8–12 months
Vegetables (freezer packaged)			8–12 months
Vegetable oil	1–3 months after opening		
Yogurt		1 month	

THE TRUTH ABOUT MOLDY CHEESE

Yes, Virginia, it is perfectly safe to cut off the moldy spots and eat the remaining cheese.

A Great Deal: Warehouse Clubs

The idea behind membership clubs like Costco, Sam's Club, and BJ's Wholesale Club is a good one: Buy in bulk and you'll save money. But there is such a thing as too much of a good thing: twelve heads of lettuce, for example, unless you're making a salad for a hundred. Still, membership in one of these clubs (each of which costs less than $50 per year) is well worth the price, especially since they sell so much more than food. You can get deals on everything from car tires to gasoline, prescriptions to vacation packages. When it comes to groceries, always keep your pantry storage capacity in mind as you shop and don't buy bulk perishables unless you know you can consume everything before it will begin to rot. "Fridge" benefit: Warehouse stores offer lots of free samples for shoppers, which means you can turn your shopping trip into a meal.

THE CASE FOR KEEPING A FULL FREEZER

Surprisingly, an empty freezer costs more to operate than one that's half to three-quarters filled with food, so keeping yours stocked will actually save you money!

■ WORTH THE MONEY

AN EXTRA FRIDGE

Is opening your fridge a frustration? Whether it happens to be empty or full, you can't easily find what you're looking for. But if you stash a small second fridge in the basement or the garage, you'll have some overflow space that helps with both problems. You can use it to store staples like an extra loaf of bread; backup bottles of essential beverages like milk, white wine, and orange juice; and the ultimate space eater, a twelve-pack of your favorite beer. If you still have the fridge from your college dorm room, just clean it up and you're in business. Otherwise, try posting an ad on Craigslist.org or poking around at a college campus on the May weekend when everyone is moving back home. Or you can purchase a new one—which will be more economical to run—from an electronics store such as Best Buy for $80 to $200, depending on its size and whether it will defrost itself.

Are Courtesy Cards Evil?

It seems like you can't go through a checkout line these days without being asked whether you have that retailer's special courtesy card. If you don't, you're sure to get the high-pressure sales pitch to apply for one. Should you?

The pros: The advantage with these cards is that they typically entitle you to a range of discounts at that store. Most grocery stores, for instance, now offer their sale prices only when a courtesy card is used. Other retailers will give you a few dollars off your total purchase every time you reach certain spending thresholds. And once you provide your mailing address on the application, you'll also receive store coupons by mail or email.

The cons: For the stores, courtesy cards are a chance to track what you buy. Run your card over the scanner, and the itemized receipt that lists everything in your shopping cart is now linked to your name and other demographic information about you. This allows the store to send you targeted mailings (which only means you're more likely to get coupons you'll actually want to use)—and to sell information about you to marketing companies (which can lead to calls from telemarketers and, some people say, is an invasion of your personal privacy).

The bottom line: So much about you is tracked by marketers already that getting courtesy cards isn't exactly opening a door that was fully closed before. Still, if you prefer to maintain your anonymity, skip the card; just smile at the checkout person when you shop and say, "I forgot my card today, will you please run yours?" It's generally store policy to do so, and you'll get the sale pricing—though not the mailed coupons—without anyone knowing who you are.

DON'T WASTE YOUR MONEY ON

. . . NONSTICK PANS.

High-quality Teflon pans cost a fortune, and the coating scrapes right off the cheap ones. What's more, Teflon can emit toxic fumes if it gets overheated. Besides, nonstick pans don't heat as evenly or cook as well as good old-fashioned cast-iron pans, which cost about $15 at the local hardware store. Pick one up at a yard sale and it'll already be seasoned from hundreds of uses. And once a cast-iron pan is seasoned, it's just as nonsticky as Teflon.

DON'T WASTE YOUR MONEY ON

Leftover Makeovers

Don't let leftovers go to waste. Many foods are just as delicious the next day—and sometimes even more so. If you want to give your leftovers new life, turn to *The Use It Up Cookbook* by Catherine Kitcho (Cumberland House), or try these simple ideas for making today's leftovers the starting points for tomorrow's meals:

- Chop cooked beef and potatoes into tiny cubes and you've got hash. Just warm and serve under poached eggs.

- Use your fingers to tear cooked poultry into bite-size pieces, toss with mayo, add cut purple grapes, and you've got yourself a terrific chicken salad.

- Crumble hamburgers, turkey burgers, or veggie burgers and reheat as the basis for make-your-own tacos. Or use them for chili con carne, pasta sauce, or sloppy joes.

- Use leftover raw ground meat to make meat loaf or meatballs.

- Toss cold pasta with broccoli, black olives, peas, carrots, and light Italian salad dressing for a delicious pasta salad.

- Turn stale bread into croutons by cubing, tossing with seasoned butter, and then toasting. Or crumble it into bread crumbs for meat loaf, meatballs, or turkey stuffing.

- Extra corn tortillas can become tortilla chips. Just cut them into wedges and fry in vegetable oil. For a healthier snack, brush them with a little olive oil and toast them in the oven.

- Use cookie crumbs as a topping for ice-cream sundaes.

- Slightly overripe fruit can be blended with ice, sugar, and orange juice to make delicious smoothies.

- Overripe bananas are ideal ingredients for banana bread.

- Slightly overripe blueberries or bananas work well in pancakes.

Grow Your Own Food

The truth is, unless it's fairly large, a vegetable garden won't yield a big enough crop to put much of a dent in your annual grocery bill. But there will be some weeks during the growing season when you're eating free food that you grew with your own hands—and it'll taste better than anything you can buy. Some of the most prolific, easy-to-grow crops are peas, lettuces, herbs, tomatoes, cucumbers, squash, and strawberries. For information about what to grow in your area and how to grow it, call a nearby university and ask for the cooperative extension service, or reach out to a local community garden organization. And to find a great selection of inexpensive seeds or seedlings so that you can grow your favorite varieties of produce—or those heirloom ones you can never afford at the organic market—go to www.johnnyseeds.com, www.burpee.com, or www.seedsofchange.com.

Good Food for Less—Farmers' Markets and CSAs

The best bargains in produce can't be found in the grocery store or bodega. You need to cut out the middlemen and the trucking companies and buy your fruits and vegetables directly from the farmer.

During the growing season, many independent growers participate in farmers' markets, where they set up card tables to proudly display and sell their products. Farmers' markets are held daily in some major cities, but in small towns and suburbs they're typically weekly events. To find a farmers' market near you, check the local newspaper, or go to www.localharvest.org and click on "Markets." That'll bring up a search engine where you can enter your zip code and see what's available.

And there's another, even more cost-effective way to buy directly from small farms: Become a shareholder. You're not actually investing in ownership of the farm, but rather buying a share of their harvest for that year. Here's how it works: You give the farm a chunk of money, say $250, at the start of the growing season; in return you get a share of each week's harvest. You may need to go to the farm to pick up your food, though some remote farms have distribution centers closer to population centers. Some programs also require members to volunteer a certain number of hours of work on the farm or distribution center.

Joining one of these programs, called community-supported agriculture (or CSA), will get you the freshest produce imaginable. And over the course of the season, you'll be getting far more food for your money than you would at the market—while supporting local farmers along the way. Like any shareholder, though, you're taking on some risk. If your farm's entire crop of tomatoes gets wiped out by a drought, for example, you won't be collecting any tomatoes in your weekly share. To find a CSA near you, go to www.biodynamics.com, www.newfarm.org, or www.localharvest.org.

THE CATCH You don't get to choose the contents of your weekly share. So be prepared to learn to cook kale, collard greens, and whatever other surprises your farmer provides.

ONE YOU NEED

SIMPLE, DELICIOUS RECIPES

Here's a cookbook that makes a big promise—simple recipes for whatever it is you want to cook, all between two covers—and it delivers: How to Cook Everything *by Mark Bittman (Wiley, 1998).*

Three Easy Ways to Save

You can cut your annual grocery bills (and help the environment to boot) simply by reducing your consumption of three disposable kitchen products:

1. Paper towels. Hang a hand towel from the handle of your refrigerator door and dry your hands on it instead of constantly hitting the paper towel roll.

2. Ziplocks. These bags are terrific for sealing leftovers and packing lunches, but Tupperware works just as well—and it can be run through the dishwasher and reused. You can even get plastic containers that are sized for sandwiches. Or throw your own Tupperware party and stock up on these storage containers practically for free.

3. Disposable dishes and utensils. Limit your use of disposables to those times when they're really the only option, such as for picnics. Then invest in thick plastic stuff instead of the flimsy paper kind, and you can handwash and reuse it a few times before sending it to the landfill.

BED, BATH, CLOSETS, LAUNDRY

Although kitchens and family rooms are where you spend much of your waking hours and entertain guests, it's the bedrooms, bathrooms, and closets that offer an oasis of privacy each morning and night. So putting in the time and effort to make these spaces comfortable and well organized is like giving yourself your own personal retreat—and there's no need to break the bank to make it happen.

Clearing Out the Clothes Closet

Organizing the clothes closet is one of those jobs that everyone dreads doing—but it actually can bring a Zen-like peace to your life. You just need to take everything out, install any new storage components you need (see "Easy Closet Makeovers" in this chapter), and then gradually load your clothes back into the closet, weeding out the deadweight as you go. There are two categories of clothes that shouldn't go back: off-season gear and stuff you're getting rid of.

Out-of-season clothes should go into storage—in your basement, attic, or garage, or at your mother-in-law's. Put folded clothes in rubber bins with snap-top lids and hanging clothes into one of those assemble-it-yourself wardrobe closets sold at the home center. Then label everything clearly (see "Worth the Money: A Label Maker" in this chapter).

Unless it's formal attire or there's some other extenuating factor—you're on an exercise kick, say, and realistically expect to fit into your smaller clothes again soon—get rid of anything that's sat unworn for a year or more. Never throw your clothes away, however. Sell them at a yard sale or donate them to charity—at a staffed office, not a drop box, so that you can get a receipt and a write-off on your income taxes. You'll have to come up with the value of the clothes, and there are no set guidelines for determining the fair value, but in general the idea is that you're writing off the amount they'd sell for at a thrift shop. A good guideline is to figure the value at about 25 percent of the item's original cost (one more reason it's always a good idea to save your receipts). Don't forget to record your mileage when driving to the drop-off location, since that's deductible, too.

WORTH THE MONEY

WORTH THE MONEY

KINDER, GENTLER CLOTHES HANGERS

The wire coat hangers that you get from the dry cleaners—or inherit with the closets in your new home—can crease and mar your clothing, and they tend to tangle together and fly off the pole willy-nilly. So it's a good idea to spend a few bucks on thicker plastic hangers, which will be gentler on your fabric and easier to keep organized on the closet pole. You can get them at any home store, or from www.hangers.com, which offers specialty hangers made of everything from plastic to cedar to satin.

Easy Closet Makeovers

A few essential accessories will help to maximize your closet space. You can get these products at home centers, or visit www.organize.com or www.stacksand stacks.com:

- Second pole. Most closets have a single pole—and a lot of wasted space under the hanging clothes. You can install a second pole underneath, or purchase one that simply hangs from the pole above.

- Canvas cubbies. These hang from the closet pole and provide soft shelves for sweaters or any other gear that needs a home.

- Shoe racks and bags. These plastic gadgets hook over the closet pole or hang over the back of a door and provide organized and accessible storage for footwear.

- Baskets and boxes. Use them to keep everything from off-season clothing to shoes organized and stowed neatly on the floor or on high shelves.

- Over-the-door racks. Ingenious contraptions that turn unused space on the backs of closet doors into serious storage for anything from shoes to purses to workout gear.

CHEAP CLOTHES

Old Navy is a Cheap Bastard's dream for filling holes in a wardrobe. The clothes are stylish and amazingly cheap, especially if you buy at the end of a season, when everything goes on sale. And the Web site (www.old navy.com) is a winner, too, because the selection is bigger than you can find in the stores (especially for petite and tall sizes), you pay only $5 in shipping no matter how much you order, and you can return anything right at your local Old Navy store.

DON'T WASTE YOUR MONEY ON

■ DON'T WASTE YOUR MONEY ON

. . . RUNNING THE CLOTHES DRYER.

When the weather is warm and dry, hanging your clothes outside will cut your electric bill (or Laundromat costs) and give them a freshness that you just can't get in a machine. String a cotton rope in a shady spot (because the sun can cause colors to fade). If the clothes feel a little stiff when you take them down, toss them in the dryer for a few minutes on the fluff cycle and they'll soften up.

What to Do about the Bathtub

If your old bathtub is scratched, chipped, pitted, rust stained, or just plain worn out, there are affordable ways to make it like new again without the mess and cost of replacement (which generally requires a total gut of the bathroom, meaning you're without that bath for weeks and spending many thousands of dollars). You can take one of two different approaches to refinishing the existing tub:

1. Line it. A contractor will come to your home and take photographs and precise measurements of your old tub. These will be used to custom-build a liner that fits it exactly. Liners are made from acrylic, which is the same material used to produce most bathtubs today. Once it's fabricated, the new

liner is delivered to your home, the drain and overflow valve are removed from your old tub, the new liner is glued in place, and then the hardware items (or new pieces) get reinstalled. You can purchase matching liners for the tub surround as well. Bath liners typically cost about $1,000, and once yours is manufactured, installation takes less than eight hours. Look in the yellow pages or contact Re-Bath (800–426–4573; re-bath.com), which has installers working in forty-seven states.

2. Refinish it. This job is done on site by spraying a new finish onto the old tub. After the bathroom has been masked off with plastic, the old tub is washed with an acid that removes the existing porcelain. Then the tub gets sprayed with a couple of coats of epoxy and finally with fresh porcelain. Once it's dry, the installer polishes the surface. This job, too, takes less than eight hours, but it has to cure afterward for twenty-four hours. The advantages of refinishing are that it's cheaper than a liner—usually less than $500—and the old character of the tub is retained. But the new porcelain coating won't be as durable as the acrylic liner. For bath refinishers in your area, look in the yellow pages.

WORTH THE MONEY

A LABEL MAKER

There's nothing like printed labels to keep everything neat and organized. Label storage bins and boxes and you won't have to rummage through them to find out what's inside. Label linen closet shelves and ensure that everything always gets put back where it belongs instead of devolving into a jumbled mess. Sure, you can do it with masking tape and an indelible marker, but you won't. Get yourself a cool label maker from an office supply store and you will.

TOWELING OFF

Here's a tip that will save you the time and expense of unnecessary laundry: Give each member of your household their own towel hook in the bathroom so they can keep track of their own towel, and wet towels won't get thrown in the hamper just because nobody knows who they belong to. Don't have enough room for more towel hooks? Buy different colors of towel for each family member.

Unfinished Business

Unfinished furniture is cheap and available in hundreds of sizes and configurations. In other words, it's the perfect solution for any bathroom that's short on cabinet and closet space. You can get a glass-doored cabinet to hang on the wall, a floor-standing cabinet, or a shelf that stands over the toilet tank. Just make sure to totally seal all the surfaces—including the back, bottom, top, and interior—with a few coats of semigloss bathroom paint to prevent moisture problems. Look for an unfinished-furniture shop near you, or order online from www.gothiccabinetcraft.com.

COMPUTERS AND HOME OFFICES

Whether you have a full-blown home office or a small desk in the corner of your bed-room, whether you work at home full-time or just pay the monthly bills, and whether you prefer doing things on a computer or the old-fashioned way, you can create an efficient and inexpensive work area.

Bargain Computers

Think you'll need to pay a lot for a new computer? Think again. Here's how to get a good deal, and where to get it:

- Buy new. This is one situation where the money you'll save by getting a preowned machine isn't worth the hassle. Unless you've got a silicone thumb (in other words, you're a techie), there's too much of a chance that an old machine is going to be buggy and problematic. And used machines don't come with tech support.

- Use a desktop. If you're really going to be computing from the road, get a laptop. Otherwise, stick with a desktop computer, which typically costs about two-thirds the price of a portable machine—and is more powerful, too.

- Buy online. Megamarts and membership clubs have good prices, but you'll likely find better prices—and certainly a greater selection—online, so at least check the Web before buying your machine.

- Comparison-shop. Go to www.cnet.com, type in whatever sort of technology you're looking for, and you'll get a list of available machines and pricing. Also check www.pcnation.com, www.compusa.com, www.jr.com, www.dell.com, and www.gateway.com.

- Look for discontinued or refurbished models. Buy a state-of-the-art machine today and it'll be outdated in six months, so you might as well save money on a machine that's slightly outdated already. And don't be afraid of refurbished equipment—which was returned and repaired by the manufacturer—as long as the manufacturer's warranty still applies.

- Call early and often. Need help setting up that printer driver or wireless router? Don't postpone making a call to tech support for help. These days most equipment comes with free tech support for a limited amount of time after you make the purchase. Take advantage of that while you can.

- Mail in the rebate form. It's not difficult, it doesn't take long, and if you do it, you'll get a check in the mail. (If you've lost the form, you can probably print out a new one from the seller's or manufacturer's Web site.)

WORTH THE MONEY

A SHREDDER

Think about all of the paperwork you throw away—from bank notices to medical forms and credit card bills. Much of that stuff contains valuable information about you, such as your account numbers, birthday, and even Social Security numbers. So literally all the information an identity thief needs in order to rob you and ruin your credit is probably in your garbage can right now—unless you shred your documents before tossing them out. Look for a shredder that's strong enough to cut through staples, old credit cards, and entire unopened junk mail envelopes.

Cheap Phone Service

A standard telephone land line can easily run you $50 a month between the phone company fees and all the taxes and surcharges. But there are other ways to go:

- Use your cell. If you carry a cell phone anyway—and get good reception in your home—there may be no need to get a landline at all. Just use the monthly minutes and free long distance you're already paying for on your cell.

- Sign up for VOIP service. If you want a landline, you still don't need to get it from the phone company. You can get phone service through your computer—assuming that you have a broadband connection. Services such as Vonage (www.vonage.com), AT&T CallVantage (www.callvantage.att.com), and Optimum Voice (www.optimumvoice.com) offer low-cost phone service (with no FCC phone-line surcharges) by routing your calls through a special adapter that they provide for free and you plug into your computer or Internet connection. Best of all, it'll allow you to check your voice mail from any Internet-connected computer.

- Use the Internet. If you have a microphone, speakers, and sound card connected to your computer—and a broadband Internet hookup—you can download software that turns your computer into a free phone. In most cases the computers at both ends of the conversation need to have the system installed, but if you upgrade with some inexpensive additional software, you can call any standard telephone number. A good place to download the necessary software is www.skype.com. (*Note:* At the time of this writing, Skype was considering a new $30 per year subscription fee for calling land- and cell lines—still, less than you might pay per month for a standard landline!)

Free Faxes

You can send and receive a limited number of faxes each month via e-mail, and can have your own dedicated fax number through a free service such as www.efax.com or www.freefax.com. Or you can pay a small monthly fee and you'll be able to send and receive an unlimited number of faxes—with a local fax number, something you won't get with the free services.

Free Dial-Up Internet Access

If you're only an occasional Internet user—or want it for infrequent e-mailing—you can get free dial-up access. The companies that offer these services do so for two reasons: In exchange for your free connection, you must watch a host of advertisements, and they hope you'll decide to upgrade to a faster connection or more than the allotted monthly access time (both of which you'll almost surely be tempted to do).

NetZero.net

Get up to ten hours per month of Internet and e-mail access for free, or upgrade to unlimited service for less than other companies charge.

BAM.com

Pay 1 cent per minute of access time (or 6.5 cents if you use the 800 line instead of a local access number).

PghConnect.com

This free dial-up service offers 400 hours a month between 7 A.M. and 7 P.M. Eastern time (plus 1,100 nighttime hours).

Freedomlist.com

Log on to search for free local or cheap regional service providers state by state—and to see comments from people who use those services.

Free Wireless Internet Access

If you have a wireless card in your laptop, you may be able to score free Internet access, because the airwaves are full of open wireless networks. It's not necessarily a good idea to piggyback onto a network that your neighbor was too lazy to secure with a password, however. Even though it's probably not illegal, so far as we've heard, and it's the service providers and not your neighbors who foot the bill for the excess traffic on the system, and even though tens of thousands of people do this without notice every single day, it's unethical and not something that we can officially condone. (The only thing we can imagine that would be worse is actually paying a monthly fee for the right to use the WiFi network at Starbucks.)

But there is nothing wrong with tapping into one of the thousands of open networks around the country that are intended as free public access points to the Internet. The cities of New York, New Orleans, and Seattle, among others, are talking about turning themselves into giant hot spots that anyone can use, and there are already a fast-growing number of free hot spots provided by governments and businesses across the country. The easiest way to find out where they are is to log on to www.wififreespot.com or www.jiwire.com. Of course, you'll need Internet access for that—try going to your local public library. It very likely will have a wireless network that you can use, and if it doesn't, it almost certainly has hardwired computer terminals available for Internet searches.

◼ GET IT FOR FREE

(OR RIDICULOUSLY CHEAP)

DIRECTORY ASSISTANCE

In this age of exorbitant fees for calling directory assistance to get a phone number, it's easy enough to log on to www.411.com, www .anywho.com, or www.yellow.com to look it up, at least when you're near a computer. Here's what to do when you're not: You can dial (800) FREE-411 (800-373-3411) from any landline or cell phone and get free directory assistance.

THE CATCH On some calls, you'll have to listen to a short advertisement. }

The Sub-$1,000 Home Office

One of the reasons that so many people work from home nowadays is that with today's technology, you can do many jobs just as efficiently from home as you can under the fluorescent lights of an office park—and you can write off part of your home utilities and office space on your taxes. If you're looking to join the ranks of virtual commuters, there are just three technology essentials you'll need—leaving plenty of money for a desk, chair, and phone in your $1,000 home office:

1. Computer. Buy online or from a megamart and you can get an excellent machine for well under $300.

2. MFP. It's a printer, copier, fax, and scanner in one machine, and you can get a brand-name model for less than $100.

3. High-speed access. If you really want to do business from home, you'll need to pay a monthly fee for DSL or cable Internet service—unless you live next door to a public library or magnanimous coffee shop (see "Free Wireless Internet Access" in this chapter).

Free Office Supplies

Recycling may be great for the environment, but it won't save you money. Reusing, on the other hand, can cut your office supply expenses. So before you throw anything in the recycling bin, think about how you may be able to reuse it and you might not need to buy:

- Notepads. Most of the office paper that you recycle still has one blank side, so cut your used paper into quarters on a paper cutter or with scissors and use binder clips to turn the stacks into free notepads.

- Envelopes. If you pay your bills online, you don't need the reply envelopes that most companies enclose with their statements. Reuse them for other mail by sticking address labels over the preprinted mailing and return addresses (and the bar codes, too).

- Stamps. One of the recent trends in direct mail marketing has been to enclose a stamp on the reply envelope. Peel off this stamp and use it for mailing something else, with the help of a glue stick if need be. (Paying your bills online is another big way to cut your need for stamps.)

- Packing materials. The paper strips in your shredder will make perfect packing material the next time you're mailing something fragile.

ATTICS, BASEMENTS, AND GARAGES

There's big money to be saved in the utilitarian parts of the home. After all, these rooms contain the house's biggest drains on the monthly bills—the heating, cooling, electrical, and plumbing services.

10 Ways to Cut Your Utility Bills

1. Turn down the thermostat. For each degree you lower it, you'll save about 3 percent on your heating costs. So drop it a few degrees and put on a sweater and some slippers. And drop it five to ten degrees at night when you'll be under a quilt anyway.

2. Move furniture. Try to arrange your furniture so that it doesn't block radiators, baseboard heating units, or hot-air registers. Otherwise you're wasting much of the heat that they're emitting.

3. Fix leaks. Leaky faucets and running toilets can waste a surprising amount of water. (A drip that fills a coffee cup in ten minutes will waste about 3,000 gallons of water in a year.) And if it's leaking hot water, you're wasting oil, natural gas, or electricity, too.

4. Open the blinds. Let the sun shine in on a clear day to pick up some free passive solar heat. Not sure it'll work? Think about how hot the interior of cars get when they're parked in the sun, even on cold days.

5. Service your system. Routine maintenance will keep your heating plant running efficiently, especially if you have an oil burner, in which case you should have your system serviced at the start of each heating season.

6. Hang insulated curtains. Thanks to a thick backing, insulated window treatments do an excellent job of sealing out cold drafts.

7. Insulate the attic. Lay rolls of fiberglass batting across the attic floor to help block heat from rising up through the roof.

8. Seal the foundation. Pick up a can of nonexpanding spray foam insulation at the home center and use it to seal any holes in the foundation, such as where plumbing pipes penetrate it.

9. Wrap the pipes. Install foam pipe insulation on any accessible heat and hot water pipes. These will not only save you money but also shorten your wait for the heat to come up and for hot water to arrive at the sink.

10. Close the damper. Did you forget to close the fireplace damper after the last fire you burned? If so, plumes of warm air are rising up the chimney and out of your house.

BARGAIN HUNTING

BARGAIN HUNTING

TIMING IS EVERYTHING

In some communities you'll be charged less for electricity that you use during off-peak hours because this lowers the utilities' demand at the busiest times, reducing their costs and the strain on their systems. If you see a discount for off-peak usage on your bills, take advantage of it by running power-hungry equipment such as your dishwasher and laundry machines at night.

Prix Fixe Heating Oil

Some oil companies offer a price cap for the entire year. Sign up with one of them in early summer and you're guaranteed that you won't pay any more than that cap for each gallon of oil that you use. If the price of oil drops, though, you'll pay less than the cap. (Or you can choose a fixed price, which will be lower than the cap price, but which you'll pay on every gallon of oil, even if prices fall.)

Another way that you can manage the high cost of oil is by signing up for a budget billing plan. Many oil companies—and gas utilities, for that matter—will estimate how much fuel you're likely to use in the coming year, multiply that number by your cap or fixed price, and then bill it to you in twelve equal chunks, once per month. That means you'll be paying for oil or gas even during the heat of the summer, but it also means you can budget a set amount every month and won't get hit with huge utility costs during the coldest times of the year. At the end of the contract, the company will compare your actual usage with what was predicted. Any amounts that you owe the company or it owes you will be folded into the monthly billing for the following year.

WHAT'S THE PAYBACK
ON ENERGY UPGRADES?

Fill out an Internet worksheet from the Lawrence Berkeley National Laboratory (http://hes.lbl.gov) and find out which energy upgrades will have the biggest impact on your bills—and whether they'll save you enough money to make them worthwhile investments.

Utility Room Storage

Here are some great ways to keep your basement or utility room tools and supplies organized for little or no money:

- Old kitchen fixtures. Don't throw out your old cabinets and countertops when you renovate the kitchen—just clean them and relocate them to your new workshop.

- Glass jars. These can be very useful in the basement. Load them with nails, screws, and other small items to keep thing sorted and visible through the clear glass.

- Basement Tupperware. The same miracle of plastic that allows for food storage containers with snap-top lids can transform your long-term storage. Unlike free cardboard boxes, large plastic bins with burpable tops will cost a few bucks each at the home center or office supply store, but their advantages make that money well spent. They're watertight, so they'll help protect what's inside from leaks and humidity—as well as bugs, dust, and general basement grime. You can even get clear bins so it's easy to see what's inside (though labeling them is still a good idea).

- Peg-Board and some hooks. Unlike the specialty systems that sell for hundreds or even thousands of dollars, you can get Peg-Board at the local hardware supply for almost nothing, and install it in just a few minutes. If you want something a little more decorative, paint it.

- A hardware cabinet. Do yourself a favor and buy one or two hanging hardware cabinets for your basement or garage. These simple rubber units are made up of multiple clear drawers that are the perfect size for storing items such as nails, screws, cable splitters, fuses, picture hooks—anything small and hard to keep track of. You can find a wide range of these cabinets at your local home center or at www.organize.com.

DON'T WASTE YOUR MONEY ON

. . . EXERCISE MACHINES.

You don't need a treadmill or a home gym to stay fit. All you need is a good pair of running sneakers (and cool-weather gear) and you can run outside just about anytime, so long as it's not icy out. And a regimen of push-ups and abdominal crunches will do wonders for your muscle tone. If you want more, invest in some simple dumbbells, which will allow you to add exercises for your back, shoulders, legs, and arms.

Better Lightbulbs

Compact fluorescent lightbulbs are nothing like those flickering tubes of the past. These screw into standard sockets, provide eye-pleasing light, and use a quarter of the energy of standard incandescent bulbs—with the same lighting power. They also last about thirteen times longer than normal bulbs before they blow out. Many electric power suppliers give them out for free or at greatly subsidized prices in order to encourage energy conservation; or you can purchase them at your local home center or www.bulbs.com.

THE CATCH

The bulbs cost about $8 each, but will save you more than that each year in electricity costs. }

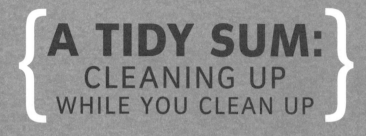

{ A TIDY SUM: }
CLEANING UP
WHILE YOU CLEAN UP

I hate housework! You make the
beds, you do the dishes—and six
months later you have to start it
all over again.

—*Joan Rivers*

A clean home feels comfortable and looks good. That's a statement that almost everyone could agree with—at least in the abstract. The reality of most households, however, is that different people have very different tolerances for messes and clutter. Whether you live with roommates, siblings, a landlord, a lover, or a spouse, there's a good chance that you'll experience some tensions over cleaning chores.

The most extreme case is when a slob and a neat freak shack up, of course, but almost any combination of people will involve mismatched sensibilities about cleanliness. Perhaps one person can't stand clothes strewn on the bedroom furniture while the other is more fanatical about dusty surfaces. In any case good housemates need to learn how to accommodate what's important to each other. They need to communicate about the household tasks and about what a fair division of labor will be. And they need to live up to their promises. The good news is that keeping a tidy home doesn't need to cost a lot of money. You can even make many of the cleaning solutions yourself.

UNCLUTTERING YOUR LIFE

It seems like the idea of organizing your home—or entire life—is on the cover of almost every "lifestyle" magazine these days. When you look inside, though, the tips tend to be about buying products, such as closet organizing systems, mail-sorting cabinets, and pantry shelf inserts. There's certainly nothing wrong with this gear if you've got cash to burn, but let's face it: Buying all the supplies in the world won't magically bring order to the chaos.

The solution to a disorganized home isn't consuming more material goods—it's taking the time to go through your things, it's clearing out the clutter, and it's rethinking the logic of how things are stored. Arrange your pantry by food type like a supermarket, for example, and you'll find it easier to cook in your kitchen. Label the shelves in your linen closet and the toolboxes on your workbench, and you'll always be able to grab what you need and put it away where you can find it next time. Organizing your home is going to take some time, but it doesn't have to cost much money—in fact it saves you money, because you don't waste time and dollars looking for or buying stuff you don't need!

The first and most important step in organizing your home is to free it of the clutter. We spend our lives accumulating stuff—clothing, magazines, books, souvenirs, decorations, tools, mementos, gadgets, paperwork, instruction manuals, leftover supplies, correspondence, and on and on. That's human nature—and it's also why our homes can so easily become cluttered messes. But now it's time to methodically go through your stuff and sort it into things you'll keep on display, things to store away in the basement or attic, things you can give to a friend or relative, things you can sell at a yard sale, and garbage. It can be an overwhelming job, especially if you've lived in the same home for a long time, but you don't have to do it all at once. You don't even have to tackle a whole room at once. Start with a drawer . . . a shelf . . . a pile.

◼ DON'T WASTE YOUR MONEY ON

. . . IONIC AIR FILTERS.

These air purifiers promise to clear the air without the noise, power consumption, or need to replace dirty filters that you face with standard room-filtering machines. But they don't do a very good job, and in some cases they add unhealthy ozone to the air inside your home.

COME 'N' GET IT!—TAG SALES

Once you've uncluttered, it's time for a tag sale—which, by the way, is no different from a "yard" sale or a "garage" sale. You'll turn your unwanted junk into cold hard cash (and you're sure to pick up a few negotiating tips from some old-time penny pinchers, because these events draw Cheap Bastards from far and wide, every one of them looking for a great deal on a diamond in the rough). Here's how to maximize your profits and—nearly as important—to make sure everything is gone at the end of the day:

- Make it a block party. You can boost your traffic and minimize your costs by talking your neighbors into throwing a whole-block tag sale. That way you can split the advertising bills and the sign-hanging chores, and if you promote the fact that multiple houses are involved, interested shoppers will turn out in droves.

- Spread the word. The key to a successful tag sale is attracting plenty of customers, and for that, just posting a sign on the front lawn the morning of the sale isn't enough (unless, perhaps, you live on a very well-traveled road). Advertise in the local newspaper at least a day before the sale. You can often put free listings in local papers. At least a week in advance, post flyers in public places such as libraries and the corner grocery store (if you're lucky enough to still have one). The morning of the sale, hang hand-made signs on the busiest street corners in the neighborhood, with arrows or an address directing passersby to your location. Make sure these signs are legible from a distance, but they really must look handmade to give a one-time-only feel to the sale. You can also post notices for free on Web

sites such as www.craigslist.org, www.garagesalehunter.com, and
www.yardsalesearch.com.

- Double date. There are two kinds of tag-sale shoppers: amateur browsers
  and professional hunters. The best way to get the most from both crowds is
  to hold a two-day sale, on Friday and Saturday. The antiques dealers and
  other seasoned shoppers will come on Friday, so you can charge higher
  prices on the first day. Then mark things down for the casual weekend
  browsers.

- Do your homework. Don't be caught selling a priceless Ming vase for four
  bucks. If you want to be sure about the value of anything you're selling,
  you can take the item to a professional appraiser. But in many cases a little
  online research will tell you all you need to know. Just attending a few tag
  sales in your area in the weeks ahead of your own can give you a good
  sense of the going rates. Or you can log on to eBay and look at recent auctions for similar products to get a sense of what they're selling for. Another
  good resource is the *Garage Sale & Flea Market Annual* (Collector Books). If
  nothing else, the research will give you a sense of whether a professional
  appraisal is warranted. Or you can try bringing your heirloom to the
  Antiques Roadshow for a free appraisal. This public television show travels
  around the country hosting appraisal events where top experts give their
  opinions about all sorts of objects. To see a list of upcoming show locations
  and to apply for tickets (which are awarded based on a lottery), go to
  www.pbs.org/wgbh/pages/roadshow.

- Clean everything and set it up in an organized and attractive fashion,
  placing small items up on card tables covered with plastic tablecloths, not
  on the ground. Group them by category, such as kitchen gear, clothing, and
  kids toys. That'll make the items look better to potential buyers—and help
  drive up prices, too.

- Be ready. You'll want at least $200 in change (ones, fives, and tens, plus coins), a calculator, a carpenter's nail apron for holding money, a permanent marker and plenty of poster board for making signs, stickers for pricing the products, and grocery bags (preferably paper) that people can use to cart home their purchases.

- Start high. You may want to get rid of the stuff, but you might as well maximize your profits, too. So price things high at the start and reduce them as the day progresses. (You don't have to mark the prices on the items, but it's a good idea to keep track of what you're hoping to get for each item rather than relying on memory.) Small appliances and other household gear will be the easiest to sell: You likely can get a third of their original purchase prices. Drop your prices 20 percent at noon; by late afternoon you can sell shopping bags for, say, $5 and let people fill them with whatever remains. If there are items you can't unload at any price, donate them to a charity for a tax write-off. Get a written receipt.

- Plan your negotiating tactics. What are you going to do when people inevitably offer lowball prices for your castaways? One good rule of thumb is to hold to the sticker price for the first third of the tag sale, meet at the midpoint between your price and their offer for the second third, and take all reasonable offers for the final third.

- Sell concessions. A lemonade stand on a hot summer day can help boost your tag sale revenue and attract additional browsers to your wares. Plus it gives kids (whether your own or your neighbors) a fun element of the sale to manage.

HOW TO CLEAN EVERYTHING

You can cut down on the time and money it takes to keep your house clean, if you know the best products and techniques for every job.

Walls

Flat paint finishes (that is, the matte textures commonly used on interior walls) should never be wetted or scrubbed because doing so can actually give that area a higher sheen so that it stands out from the rest of the wall. For those surfaces and old wallpapers, try a Gonzo Sponge (see "Three Must-Have Cleaning Tools" in this chapter). Glossy paints (often used on woodwork and trim) and recently installed wallpaper, however, can be wiped with a sponge dampened by water mixed with a drop or two of dishwashing soap.

Bare Floors

Brooms are simple and inexpensive tools, but they're not the best way to keep floors clean—they kick up too much dust. You're better off using a vacuum without a beater brush and with a high-efficiency filter to trap the dust and prevent it from going airborne. Also, don't wet-mop wood floors, because the moisture can damage them: Use a damp mop and a solution of ½ cup white vinegar added to 1 gallon water.

Carpets

The very nature of carpeting makes it almost impossible to remove all of the dirt and grime that works its way into the fibers. But here's how to get your rugs as clean as possible:

- Don't get them dirty in the first place. Have everyone remove their shoes at the door to your home and you'll reduce the amount of debris that gets tracked onto them. Also, don't eat meals over carpeting.

- Vacuum messes right way. You need a vacuum with a beater brush, and you need to pass over each section of carpet at least four times (out and back, out and back). Also, don't always vacuum the same way: Switch where you stand and in which direction you move the vacuum. You can also occasionally flip an area rug, vacuum under it, and vacuum its backside as well. To deodorize, skip the scented powders and simply sprinkle some baking soda over the pile about half an hour before vacuuming.

- Steam them clean. When they're stained or grimy, area rugs can be sent out for professional cleaning, but you'll need to bring the equipment into your home for wall-to-wall carpeting. You'll save money by renting a machine at the home center and doing it yourself instead of hiring a professional service.

Windows

Washing windows will make your entire home look better—and feel cleaner and brighter, too. Luckily, you don't need to buy a truckload of paper towels and glass cleaner for the job. Use crumpled newspaper, which won't leave streaks or lint behind and will actually help the window repel dirt in the future. Make your own cleaning solution by adding either 2 tablespoons ammonia or 3 tablespoons white vinegar to a clean spray bottle filled with warm water.

Upholstery

Look at the care tag on upholstered furniture. If there's a w on it, you can clean it yourself. Use a clean sponge and a mixture of warm water and Woolite (at a ratio of about a gallon to a couple of teaspoons). Dip the sponge in the solution, wring it dry, and gently dab it on dirt or stains in the fabric. Allow the fabric to dry thoroughly before reassembling the cushions. If there's no w on the tag, sorry, but you're going to have to call in a professional upholstery-cleaning service.

Curtains

Vacuum them regularly using the attachment with the brush on the end. Pay special attention to the top edge and the interiors of the pleats. For stain removal and deep cleaning, send the curtains to the dry cleaner.

Blinds

Some people dunk their blinds in a tub of water to make washing easier, but soaking the cords can cause mildew and mold. You're better off simply vacuuming the blinds thoroughly, then cleaning with a rag dampened in water mixed with a few drops of dishwashing liquid. Wipe both sides of each slat, one at a time.

Computers

To remove dust, fingerprints, and coffee stains from your computer, use a rag that's been slightly dampened with a mixture of half white vinegar and half water. Make sure not to drip into the keyboard or any other openings, and use a cotton swab for hard-to-reach crevices.

Pots and Pans

To scour dirty pans, use baking soda, which is slightly abrasive and yet gentle on the metal and totally nontoxic.

SHARING CHORES

Whether you live with roommates or a bedmate, there's a good bet that there have been—or will be—tensions over chores. Someone is doing more cleaning than someone else, or maybe someone isn't doing any chores at all. But that doesn't mean you need to kick anyone out of the house, hire someone to do all the chores, nag one another, or otherwise break up an otherwise good living arrangement. Here are some tips on coming up with a household division of labor that really works:

- The gender gap. Women do better than two-thirds of the chores around most houses. We learned this division of labor from our parents, who learned it from theirs, and so forth. But in previous generations, women usually didn't work outside the home, while in many households nowadays the women are bringing home the nitrate-free turkey bacon, too. In such cases it's simply not fair to fall back on ancient norms for who does the cleaning.

- Give the men credit. On the other hand, men often don't get credit for the jobs they do because, in many households, the work men gravitate toward is less routine than women's chores. For example, perhaps the woman does the laundry, which is a weekly or even daily chore. The man mows the lawn, but only in summer. He shovels the walk, but only after it snows. And he fixes things, but only when they break. Give him credit for what he does even if the work isn't as regular.

- Have a meeting. Don't try to settle disputes over who does what when you're angry. And don't nag. Instead have a sit-down when everyone is in a good mood. Discuss your feelings and split up the responsibilities equitably.

- Play cards. One good trick is to list each major household chore on an index card. Then deal out the cards to each housemate. You can either shuffle the deck first and randomize the assignments, or dole them out based on who prefers to do what in your home. Hang the assignments under each housemate's name on a bulletin board or the refrigerator as a frequent and public reminder of whose responsibilities are whose. Then you can reshuffle the cards—and hence the jobs—every week or month.

- Create cleaning hour. You might also schedule an hour here or there when all members of the house do their chores at the same time. Blast some fast-paced music on the stereo, break out a six-pack, and turn it into a fun event.

- Hire help. If there are some chores that just don't seem to get done by anyone or that cause a lot of household stress—from cleaning the bathroom to dusting the baseboards to shoveling the driveway—consider hiring a professional to do those tasks.

■ **WORTH THE MONEY**

A CLEANING PERSON

Paying someone to clean your house is, without a doubt, money well spent. Not only do you get a clean home, but you also reduce tensions among housemates. And you don't need to spend a fortune to make it happen. You could hire someone to clean just the bathrooms and kitchen each week, someone to clean the entire house every other week, or someone to do seasonal deep cleanings—whatever fits your budget and your needs. Prices vary widely depending on where you live, how big your home is, how messy it is, and whom you hire, but for ballpark figures, expect to pay anywhere from $50 to $100 for a full housecleaning.

THE CATCH

Finding a good cleaning person isn't always easy. You'll need to get referrals in order to find someone who does a thorough job—and whom you can trust in your home.

THE TRUTH ABOUT INDOOR AIR QUALITY

All it takes is a ray of sunshine viewed at the right angle, and you can see that the air inside your home is filled with tiny particles of dust. And those are just the pieces that are large enough for you to see. At any given moment there are an infinitesimal number of microscopic bits of pet dander, pollen, skin cells, lint, and other particles polluting the air inside your home. But you don't need to run out and get an air-purifying machine. Here's how to clean the air you breathe:

- Keep your house clean. Vacuum regularly. Use a damp rag to clean the out-of-the-way places where dust collects, such as baseboards, the top of the refrigerator, and windowsills (especially important when you open the windows for the first time each spring).

- Air it out. The best way to clear the air is to open some windows. Just pick your moments. Don't do it on high-pollen days, for example, especially if someone in the home has allergies. And ideally, you should do it when the weather is dry and sixty-five to seventy-five degrees, so you don't add to the strain on your heating or air-conditioning systems.

- Put the filter where you need it most. High-efficiency filters such as HEPAs have become popular accessories these days, but most people don't have them where they'll do the most good. Putting a high-efficiency filter on a central air-conditioning system, for example, is an excellent way to prevent the ducts from becoming dirty, but in most cases it won't act as a very effective purifier for your indoor air, because not enough of the air actually passes through the system. You'll get better results from a freestanding room filter, which will process all the air in the room—but only that room. In actuality, the most important location for a HEPA filter—and most affordable, too—is on your vacuum. Without one, a vacuum can be the number one source of indoor air pollution in your home, because poorly filtered units spew out dust and debris with the exhaust air. With a HEPA filter, however, your vacuum can efficiently pick up dirt and deposit almost every single speck of it in a disposable bag.

CLEANING SUPPLIES THAT WON'T CLEAN YOU OUT

The aisles of grocery stores and home centers are overflowing with specialty products, each one marketed for a specific cleaning chore. But you don't need a different bottle of detergent for every job. There are really just a few essentials—some of which you can even make yourself.

All-Purpose Cleaners

Two inexpensive kitchen ingredients that you already have in your cabinet can be used for dozens of household cleaning projects: vinegar and baking soda.

The word *vinegar* means "sour wine"—and that's just what vinegar is, wine that's been exposed to bacteria and allowed to ferment a second time. As disappointing as a soured bottle of wine is, vinegar itself has an amazing range of uses far beyond dressing salads or pickling cucumbers.

Baking soda is a mineral, sodium bicarbonate, that's mined from a giant deposit in Wyoming, purified, and boxed up as a baker's leavening tool. But its odor- and acid-fighting properties make it useful for countless cleaning projects, too.

- To get glassware spot-free in the dishwasher, pour ½ cup vinegar into the rinse cycle dispenser before each load.

- Clean the internal parts of your coffeemaker by pouring 1 cup vinegar into the water reservoir and turning the machine on. Once the vinegar has run through, fill the tank with water and run it through twice. (Check the owner's manual first to make sure a vinegar treatment isn't prohibited.)

- Clean wood floors by damp-mopping them with a solution of ½ cup white vinegar added to 1 gallon water.

- Wash windows with a mixture of 3 tablespoons white vinegar added to a clean spray bottle filled with warm water.

- Clean your computer using a rag that's been slightly dampened with a mixture of half white vinegar and half water.

- To combat odors in the basement, or any room, leave a bowl of vinegar in the space. Or you can wash down the offending surfaces with a mixture of 1 cup vinegar, 1 cup ammonia, ¼ cup baking soda, and 1 gallon water.

- To clean and deodorize drains, pour 1 cup baking soda and 1 cup hot vinegar (heat in the microwave) into a closed drain, let stand 5 minutes, and then flush with hot tap water to clean and deodorize. (Or pour the mixture into a running garbage disposal before flushing with hot water.)

- To clean the toilet bowl, pour in 1 cup vinegar and 1 cup borax. Let this stand for about an hour before scrubbing.

- To get clothes smelling fresh, reduce static cling, and fully rinse away the laundry detergent, add ¼ cup vinegar to the rinse cycle.

- To keep the fridge and freezer smelling clean, place one opened box of baking soda in each. Replace the old boxes at the start of each new season.

- To fight kitchen fires, keep a large open box of baking soda handy as a backup for your fire extinguisher. Unlike water, it's a safe means for fighting both electrical and grease fires.

- To freshen carpet odors, sprinkle baking soda on the pile and, if necessary, work it in with a broom. Let it stand overnight before vacuuming it up.

- To clean grungy pots and pans, scour them with baking soda, which is slightly abrasive yet gentle on the metal and totally nontoxic.

DON'T WASTE YOUR MONEY ON

■ **DON'T WASTE YOUR MONEY ON**

. . . BUYING TOO MUCH DISH SOAP.

In most dishwashers you need only about a teaspoon of powdered deter-gent to do the job. (Don't use liquid, because it can damage the dish-washer over time.) And for washing by hand you only need about a tea-spoon of dish soap for a whole sink full of warm water.

■

The Cleaning Kit Trick

Are your cleaning supplies a jumbled mess under the kitchen sink? That's a sure-fire way to discourage yourself from grabbing a few of them and embarking on a much-needed housekeeping project some quiet Sunday afternoon. Here's a simple technique for keeping your supplies organized and making cleaning proj-ects easier: Purchase a few buckets at a home center and use each one to create a different cleaning kit by storing the supplies needed for a specific cleaning project. You can create kits for the bathroom, the kitchen, dusting, windows, and so forth.

Three Must-Have Cleaning Tools

1. Swiffer disposable mop heads. They cost a few bucks, but they make mopping painless. You don't have to wet the mop, wring it out, or wash it off when you're done. Just grab a premoistened sheet, stick it on the special mop head, and go. When the head gets dried out or dirty, toss the sheet and grab another one. They're available at any drugstore, supermarket, or home center.

2. Gonzo Wonder Sponge. Rub this dry foam latex sponge over fabrics, walls, and furniture and it picks up dirt, lint, and pet hair. Then you can wash the sponge in the sink and use it again. Look for these at home stores or from www.gonzocorp.com.

3. Weiman Stainless Steel Cleaner & Polish. The stainless-steel look isn't only for high-end appliances anymore. It's everywhere. And keeping these surfaces (which are actually made of aluminum) clean and free of water spots and fingerprints is easiest with this specialized cleaner. Just spray it on and then wipe it away. You can get the spray at home stores or from www.weiman.com.

DUSTING—
IT'S NOTHING TO SNEEZE AT

This much-hated chore isn't so hard if you follow these basic tips:

- Choose the right tool. Feather dusters tend to spread dust into the air. Paper towels can scratch soft wood and leave lint behind on shiny surfaces. A lamb's-wool duster is the perfect tool, but there's something you can get for free that works nearly as well—old 100 percent cotton T-shirts and underwear. To dust intricate objects such as a chandelier, try an unused paintbrush.

- Work from the top down. Wrap a cloth around a broom handle to reach cobwebs on the ceilings, then use your T-shirt rag and gradually move to the window trim, furniture, and baseboards. And don't forget about lightbulbs, houseplant leaves, lamp shades, and picture frames.

- Make repairs. If you notice scratches in unpainted woodwork as you dust, you can hide the damage with a crayon. Look through a large box of children's crayons—the kind with 200 colors is ideal—and choose the one that best matches the wood. Just rub it over the scratch to fill it in.

- Make your own dust repellent by combining 2 cups warm water with ½ cup liquid fabric softener. Pour this into a spray bottle and use it for high-dust areas such as coffee tables and the top of the refrigerator. But don't spray it onto electronics—dust those with used dryer sheets, which will have a similar effect.

DON'T WASTE YOUR MONEY ON

■ DON'T WASTE YOUR MONEY ON

. . . PLUG-IN SCENTS.

Those contraptions and other artificial fragrances simply mask bad odors. And it's easy enough to remove most unappealing smells, whether they're in a basement, closet, or bathroom. The secret is plain old grocery store white vinegar. You can leave a bowl of vinegar out to combat odors, or wash down the offending surfaces with a mixture of 1 cup vinegar, 1 cup ammonia, ¼ cup baking soda, and 1 gallon water.

Well-Filtered Vacuums

Look for a vacuum with a high-efficiency filter—which means getting one that's new or at least no more than a few years old. Upright models are cheaper and easier to store than canisters, and they tend to do better on carpets. But canisters work better for bare floors, as well as stairs and upholstery. Make sure to compare the total weight and the decibel levels of the machines as well.

{ **GROWTH FUNDS:** A DIRT CHEAP APPROACH TO YARD WORK }

Your first job is to prepare the soil.
The best tool for this is your
neighbor's motorized garden tiller. If
your neighbor does not own a garden
tiller, suggest that he buy one.

—*Dave Barry*

No matter what condition your yard is in—maybe the grass is brown, the shrubs are overgrown, or the whole place is a weedy mess—transforming it into something you're proud of doesn't have to cost a lot of money. You don't need an army of landscapers to bring truckloads of new plantings. You don't even need a green thumb. Just do some basic pruning, tending, and planting; give everything a couple of growing seasons to mature; and your yard will be new again. Best of all, you can tackle the job little by little, and the skills are simple to pick up once you understand some basic principles. So here's how to create a beautiful outdoor space, whether you have an acre, a postage-stamp yard, a terrace, or just a few sunny window boxes.

MAKING OVERGROWN SHRUBS NEW AGAIN

Just because the shrubs along your foundation are overgrown and leggy doesn't mean you have to rip them out and start over or live with a shroud of scraggly 10 foot bushes around your home. If you're patient, you can renew many shrubs by cutting them way back and letting them regrow. Take rhododendrons, spireas, honeysuckles, beautybushes, Indian currants, snowberries, or privets down to stubs a foot or so off the ground, for example, and they will send out new shoots that become nice bushes in a couple of years. If you don't want a barren landscape while you wait, just cut back a third of the shrub's branches each year for the next three. This kind of pruning is best done in late spring or summer. Meanwhile, here's how to keep the problem from happening again:

- These days you can get shrubs that will never grow any larger than you want them. So when you're planting along the foundation, around a patio, or anywhere that you want a compact plant, look for dwarf species that will max out at 2 or 3 feet tall and wide when they're mature, then plant them that far away from each other and half that distance from the house. They won't need much pruning at all.

- For plants with branching trunks (versus numerous thin twigs coming up from the ground), there are two crucial rules of pruning so they don't become leggy. First, don't use hedge trimmers; instead use hand pruners so that you can cut some branches longer than others, creating a more naturalistic plant shape and allowing sunshine to get inside so foliage can grow there instead of just forming around the perimeter of the plant. Second, taper the plant so it's narrowest at the top and slightly wider at the base. This ensures that the upper branches won't shade out the lower branches and prevent leaves from growing on them. Such pruning should be done shortly after the shrub flowers.

■ GET IT FOR FREE

(OR RIDICULOUSLY CHEAP)

THAT NICE FARM SMELL

If you live near any small farms—or zoos—ask them whether they have manure that you can dig and use in your garden. Just make sure that it's already been composted so that it's hygienic and will be beneficial for your plantings.

■

MAKE YOUR OWN FERTILIZER

There is no better plant food than compost—and this stuff is free. Nothing could be simpler to make yourself. Just start a compost heap in an out-of-the-way place somewhere in your yard and toss kitchen and yard waste onto the pile. Add a little water and stir occasionally. The mixture will gradually rot and become a fertile soil-like material that you can use for planting or simply sprinkle around the bases of existing plants.

The Container

The simplest approach is to bang four stakes into the ground and then wrap them with chicken wire, but that will require using a shovel to turn the mix now and then. You can also buy a host of different plastic bins designed to make composting even easier. Some you simply spin to mix the organic brew inside, while others have removable slats that allow you to shovel out the best compost from the bottom of the pile. Some cities and regional environmental groups sell discounted composters as a way to reduce solid waste, so check with your town's public works department. Or you can find good selections at www.composters.com, www.gardeners.com, or www.plowhearth.com.

The Ingredients

Good compost requires two types of household waste: green and brown. Green materials include grass clippings and kitchen vegetable scraps. Brown materials include dead autumn leaves and other yard debris. Ideally, you want a ratio of 2 parts brown materials to 1 part green. For more information about ingredients, see www.compostguide.com.

The Process

Compost actually gets hot as it decomposes, and that kills any bacteria or other pathogens in the waste. Some composting bins help keep the pile hot by insulating it slightly. Still, compost needs oxygen and water, so you'll need to turn the pile and keep it damp. A pitchfork will be far more effective than a shovel for this job. Depending on what you put in, how diligent you are with water and turning, and in what season you're composting, making compost takes six weeks to six months.

■ GET IT FOR FREE

COMPOST AND MULCH

If your town collects leaves each fall, you're probably already taking advantage of that free service. But you may be missing out on another one: the compost that your town makes from those leaves. In many cases residents can get free compost—as well as mulch made from the ground-up branches cut by town crews—either for free or for a nominal charge. Aside from being the best deal in town, these products have the advantage of being made entirely from local yard debris. Thus you won't run the risk of introducing foreign insects or diseases, which can happen if you buy bagged products that were harvested hundreds of miles away.

GOOD GRASS CHEAP

Even if you wanted to spend $500 to $1,000 a year to have a lawn service transform your scraggly grass into lush green turf worthy of the PGA Tour, there are good reasons not to. For one thing, the nutrients that run off chemically treated lawns can cause algae blooms in nearby streams and wetlands, wreaking havoc on the ecological balance of the plants and animals that live there. For another, the weed killers can be unhealthy to people and pets who spend time on the lawn. And the truth is, all that fertilizer and herbicide isn't necessary if you keep your lawn healthy by using the proper techniques for routine care.

Mowing

Regular cutting is essential to the health of a lawn, but it's easy to make mistakes that damage the grass:

- The most common misstep is shearing the grass too short, which can shock the plants and make them more susceptible to drought. Never cut the grass shorter than 2 inches or take more than a third of its height away in a single mow.

- Don't bag your clippings, which is basically just carting away nutrients and moisture. Instead, use a mulching mower to chop up the cut ends and recycle their water and nutrients to the turf; that'll reduce the need for future feedings by about a third, saving you money—and the hassle of repeatedly dumping the grass-catching bag, too.

- Never mow the grass when it's wet. This dulls the mower blade, causing it to tear the grass instead of slicing cleanly through. It makes the clippings clump up and sit on the surface rather than getting chopped finely and settling into the turf.

Feeding

Most lawn fertilizers are almost all nitrogen, which is the nutrient that "greens up" the grass. But it's actually phosphorus that creates truly healthy lawns, because it promotes root growth. Buy your fertilizer at a local nursery, and ask for a balanced mix that will promote root growth. (All commercial fertilizers contain three nutrients—nitrogen, phosphorus, and potassium—the quantities of which are noted, in that order, by three numbers on the bag.)

Watering

During the heat of summer, lawns need at least an inch of water a week, and it's easy enough to measure rainfall totals simply by leaving a straight-edged cup out in the weather.

- If Mother Nature falls short, supplement with a sprinkler in the early morning. Less moisture will be wasted through evaporation than during the heat of midday, and the grass will have time to dry before dark, when blades that are wet can become diseased.

- It's better to water heavily only once or twice a week than to do a quick sprinkle more frequently: Deep watering encourages roots to grow downward in search of moisture. Still, don't overwater, either. Stop the flow before water begins puddling on the surface.

Weeding

Nobody likes weeds, but it helps to understand that lawn grass really isn't the natural state of things. Left to its own devices, your yard would not be turf; it would be a mix of other plants, such as trees, native ground covers, dandelions, and all the other things we call weeds. You can beat these back with chemicals, but if you don't feel comfortable with that—for financial, ecological, or health reasons—here's what you can do:

- The healthier your lawn is, the better able it will be to defend itself from weeds (and pests) naturally. So you can judiciously use chemical weed killers for a few seasons to give the lawn the upper hand, you can hand-pull weeds that appear in early spring before they spread, and/or you can learn to live with some weeds in your lawn.

- There is one weed that isn't so benign, however: crabgrass. This wide-bladed grass actually doesn't even look like a weed, but it's an invasive annual, meaning that it gradually overtakes your turf grass during the growing season and then dies off in winter, leaving you with dirt where your lawn had been. Luckily, there's a safe way to block crabgrass in spring: Get a preemergent crabgrass inhibitor at your local nursery center and spread it over the soil to create a physical barrier that inhibits crabgrass germination.

PUSH MOWERS

Unless your yard is big, a push mower will save you a lot of money compared with a gas or electric machine—not only for the initial purchase, but also for fuel and tune-ups. These mowers do a terrific job of trimming the grass, and will save you the cost of a gym membership, too!

WORTH THE MONEY

THE BEST GRASS SEED YOU CAN GET

Never skimp on grass seed. The cheap stuff contains grass varieties that are harder to grow—and weed seeds, too. Instead, go to a local nursery and buy its premium seed mix, which should have a handful of named varieties known to perform well in your area.

Fall Maintenance

If you live in a climate where winter means icy temperatures, autumn is the best time to work on your grass. In addition to the tendency of plants to be growing roots at this time of year, and the relatively mild and wet weather, the big advantage to fall lawn care is that weed seeds don't germinate in fall but grass seeds do, so any soil you expose now can get a nice coverage of new grass before the weeds try to invade.

- Every year or two it's a good idea to aerate, a process that involves cutting 3-inch-deep plugs out of the lawn, which loosens compacted soil and helps nutrients and water reach the roots. You can even sprinkle compost over the grass after aerating so that it can work its way into the holes to bolster the depleted topsoil underneath. If your yard is small and you have time, you can don a pair of aerating sandals (in sizes 6 to 10 at www.gardeners.com), which have spikelike cleats, and walk around to do the job. Or you can rent a power aerator by the day at a home center, and why not share the cost with a couple of neighbors?

- While you're at it, rent a dethatcher, too. This machine literally chops up the lawn, tearing out the dead roots that, with many grass types, otherwise become a matted layer that chokes the lawn to death. A machine rents for about $50 to $100 a day and will give you a healthier lawn for years to come.

- Fall is also the time to seed, again because of the absence of weed germination.

■ DON'T WASTE YOUR MONEY ON

. . . LAWN MOWER REPAIRS.

Nine times out of ten, when you pull out your lawn mower in spring and it won't start (or it runs roughly), the problem isn't the mower—it's the old gas. Gas actually breaks down over time, and you can pull your arm out of its socket trying to start a mower on stale gas. So remove the old gas using a gasoline siphon and take it to a hazardous waste collection facility for disposal. You can avoid this problem by buying your mower gas in 1- or 2-gallon portions rather than larger quantities. Also, run the mower until the gas tank is dry after the last mow of fall.

THE CATCH You can't avoid the mower mechanic altogether; it's a good idea to bring all gas-powered yard equipment in for a tune-up now and then. }

WATER WATER ALL AROUND, WHY PAY FOR IT?

Water is a vital natural resource—and a costly one, too. In some Boston-area towns, for example, folks pay nearly $10 for every 100 cubic feet of water, including sewer fees, which are calculated based on how much water you use, even if that water gets sprayed on the lawn and never goes down the drain. At that price the cost of the 10,000 gallons the typical household sprays on its yard each year is more than $130. Even if the water spraying out of your hose doesn't cost that much, it does consume a precious environmental resource. Plus, tap water is loaded with chlorine and other chemicals that are designed to make it safe for human consumption but are actually harmful to the landscape.

There is a better way: Collect the water from your roof, an ancient technique that yields free clean water for your yard. The roof of a modest-size house gets doused with about 400 gallons of water for every ½ inch of rain that falls, and you already have a collection system that gathers all of that water—the gutters. So attach one of your downspouts to a rain barrel, and let those gutters gather H_2O for watering purposes.

You can get rain barrels that will hold from twenty gallons (enough for urban terraces, window boxes, and houseplants) to a hundred. When it's time to water, just connect a hose to the spigot on the bottom of the barrel and let gravity act as your pump. It won't have the power (or the capacity) to drive your lawn sprinkler, but it can hydrate shrubs, flower beds, and vegetable gardens.

Some cities and regional environmental organizations give away rain barrels for free or sell them at discounted prices in order to reduce the demand on the public water supply. But you can also buy them, starting at about $100, at www.cleanair gardening.com, www.gardeners.com, and www.rainwatersolutions.com. Remember to order some mosquito control pellets to add to the water, which will otherwise provide an ideal breeding ground for their larvae. Some people just pour a few tablespoons of vegetable oil over the surface to suffocate the larvae, but because of concerns about mosquitoes carrying West Nile virus, the Environmental Protection Agency recommends the chemical treatments, which are essentially nontoxic to people.

■ DON'T WASTE YOUR MONEY ON

DON'T WASTE YOUR MONEY ON

. . . A BIG GAS GRILL.

Why does everyone think they need those gleaming gas grills with burners for boiling corn and cooking surfaces big enough to roast a side of beef? Such giants may look cool, but they don't do much for the meat. To get real barbecue flavor, you need a quaint little thing called charcoal. Gas won't do it. And that's why the best grill you can get is still a Weber charcoal kettle (available at any hardware store, home center, or www.barbecues.com). Then splurge for lump hardwood charcoal (from www.hastybake.com or www.barbecue-store.com) instead of the standard briquettes, which are chock-full of lighter fluid and industrial additives.

POWER PLANTS AND SUPPLIES

It starts innocently enough. You hit the nursery to pick up some flowers for the yard. The next thing you know, you've filled your trunk with shrubs and groundcovers that you just can't live without—and emptied your wallet of hundreds of your hard-won dollars. It doesn't have to be that way. Any plant you want can be had for just pennies—or even for free—if you know where to look.

Why Buy Plants?

To paraphrase an old riddle: Which came first, the plant or the seed? In fact, many plants sold at nurseries and home centers didn't start out as seeds at all; they were propagated from cuttings. It's a quicker process that gives growers more control over the results. And you can do the same thing, turning small cuttings into free plants for the yard or for your indoor pots. Etiquette—or perhaps discretion—calls for asking permission before hacking off a piece of your neighbor's prized crepe myrtle, of course.

The process is simple and you can use it to create your own new tree or shrub, although you might want to refer to a gardening manual or a state extension service (such as www.muextension.missouri.edu) for more information about how to handle specific plant types. (For perennials, the method is different: Simply dig up a few of the plants, roots and all, and plant them in your own yard.)

1. Cut about 5 inches of healthy new growth from a tree, shrub, or virtually any woody ornamental plant. Try to avoid buds and flowers, or simply remove them (so that the plant can focus its energy on establishing roots).

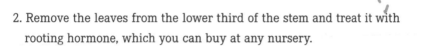

2. Remove the leaves from the lower third of the stem and treat it with rooting hormone, which you can buy at any nursery.

3. Place the cut end a few inches deep in a pot of sterile soil, and then water, covering the pot with plastic to maintain humidity and locating it in indirect sunlight.

4. Allow the newly rooted stem to establish itself into a thriving plant before gradually acclimating it to the outside world and then transplanting it into its permanent home.

THE CATCH It'll be years before you'll have a full-size crepe myrtle of your own. If you need a big tree faster than that, refer to the list of affordable mail-order sources for plants in this chapter. }

Gardening from Seed

There are also plenty of plants—especially annual flowers, vegetables, and other single-season growers—that you can start from seeds, which cost just pennies a packet. This can be done under grow lights indoors (purchase at www.aero garden.com) if you want to have seedlings ready to transplant outdoors as soon as the time is right. In many cases you can simply plant the seeds outside and let them perform their magic right where you want them. Check the seed packet for specific requirements and any good gardening manual for basic instructions.

Seed and Plant Swaps

Another way to get yard and houseplants for free is to trade your extra plants and seeds with other gardeners. You can do this by attending one of the hundreds of swaps that are held around the country (ask around or check your local newspaper for listings) or, in the case of seed swaps, by logging on to a gardeners' forum on the Internet. See www.garden.org (click on "Seed Swap") and www.seed savers.org (which charges a small fee).

What You Should Know about Perennials and Annuals

Most of the flowers that you can plant in your yard fall into one of two categories: annuals and perennials. Find out which a plant is, and you'll know just what kind of return you're going to get on your investment.

Plant a perennial once and it'll be in your landscape for years to come, blooming like clockwork at the same period of each season, with the flowers lasting for a couple of weeks or more. These can be trees, shrubs, ground covers, or bulbs. Many can be grown indoors as well, but they need to be put in a cold environment such as a basement or freezer for a couple of months or so in order to give them a period of winter dormancy.

Annuals, on the other hand, will die at the end of a single growing season, but that doesn't mean that they're a bad investment. For one thing, they cost a lot less than perennials; for another, they generally spread out to fill an entire bed or planter after a few weeks. They also flower profusely and continuously for many weeks—or in some cases for the entire growing season.

FLOWERS IN WINTER

Did you know that you can dig up your spring-flowering bulbs—from crocuses to daffodils to tulips—bring them inside, and get them to bloom in pots in winter? It's called forcing bulbs, *but it doesn't really involve any coercion.* Tricking bulbs *would be a more accurate name, because what you do is simply place the bulbs in the refrigerator or an unheated garage for about ten weeks before bringing them into the warm air of the house. This process creates a period of winter dormancy and then a spring warm-up, and it makes the plants bloom profusely. Then, when spring really does arrive, you can return them to your garden—and the real cycle of seasons. For instructions on forcing different kinds of bulbs, see www.hort.wisc.edu/mastergardener/Features/bulbs/forcebulbs/force bulbs.htm.*

There is also a middle ground—or maybe it's the best of both worlds. Some plants that are sold as annuals—the mums you can get at every supermarket in autumn, for example, as well as many varieties of daisy, verbena, snapdragon, and pansy—are actually perennials. Plant them in the ground and they'll return in spring. Many true annuals will return, too. Let their flowers turn to seeds, and they'll repropagate themselves.

TREES FOR THE ASKING

We all know that planting trees is good for the environment. But planting one along the street has a lot more benefits than that. It instantly beautifies your home, reduces the traffic noise inside your house, and increases your property value. It also improves the streetscape, which is one reason why many municipalities will plant street trees along your frontage either for free or at the town's wholesale cost. The other reason is that it allows town tree wardens to recommend the trees they want to plant—thus creating appealing variety from house to house and choosing species that won't become a maintenance hassle by growing up into the power lines. By the way, in most cases towns and utilities will take care of cutting dead limbs from any trees planted between the sidewalk and street if they become a hazard, so you may not need to pay a tree service. To find out about your town's street tree planting and pruning programs, call the public works department.

Yard-Work Must-Haves

A few simple, inexpensive products can make your yard work—indeed, everything you do in the outdoors—a pleasure.

- Tecnu. An unfortunate reality of clearing an overgrown yard is that all too often you wake up the next morning with a terrible rash from poison ivy, oak, or sumac. The rash can spread over your body and even onto other members of the family because it's caused by an invisible oil that sticks to your skin even when you wash up—and then spreads onto other parts of your body, bedmates, sheets, and towels. Tecnu is a special soap that removes the oil from your skin. Use it as directed when you come inside from any outdoor clearing work and you won't get the rash. It's available at any drugstore, or in bulk bottles and travel-size packets from www.gemplers.com.

- Fish emulsion. Forget about Miracle-Gro and other chemical fertilizers. This is the only fertilizer you need for your lawn, flowers, and vegetable gardens. There's nothing better for your plants—especially for vegetables—and it's totally organic.

  THE CATCH Things will be a little smelly for a day or so after you apply it. After all, it's made from fermented fish oil. }

- Insecticidal soap. Here's another essential tool from the organic gardener's bag of tricks. As the name implies, it's a soap that acts as an insecticide for many plant-eating pests. If you have plants that are getting eaten, simply spray the nontoxic liquid onto leaves—coating both the plants and the bugs thoroughly—and it'll kill many types of infestations. Yet it won't harm the plant, environment, pets, or kids—and this one doesn't smell bad at all. You don't even have to buy the insecticidal soap sold at nurseries; you can make your own from a 2 to 3 percent mixture of regular dish or hand soap and water. If the mix doesn't work, try a different brand of dish soap.

A Yard and Garden Source Guide

The seeds and plants that you can buy via mail order are cheaper than what's available at the local nursery. Plus, there's a wider selection and fresher stock than what you'll find at the local home center.

Bluestone Perennials (800–852–5243, www.bluestoneperennials.com)

Bluestone is a well-regarded mail-order supplier of bulbs, perennials, ground covers, shrubs, trees, vines, and ornamental grasses.

Burpee (215–674–4900, www.burpee.com)

This 125-year-old company has probably been the top national seller of seeds for every year of its existence. The company breeds its own varieties and offers a huge selection of flowers, vegetables, and other garden plants.

Gardener's Supply Company (800–944–2250, www.gardeners.com)

This is the place to go for garden tools, supplies, and decorative accessories. You'll find a complete selection of composters, for example, as well as everything you need to create your own drip irrigation system. You can even buy greenhouses here—as well as organic fertilizer and the very best gardening hand tools around.

Indiana Berry & Plant Co. (800–295–2226)

A complete selection of fruit trees and berry plants you can have delivered to your door for a fraction of the price you'll pay at the local nursery.

Johnny's Selected Seeds (800–738–6314, www.johnnyseeds.com)

A wide selection of seeds and bulbs for virtually any plant you want to grow, plus tools, how-to books, and other supplies.

Lilypons Water Gardens (800–999–5459, www.lilypons.com)

This is the place to order everything you need to create a backyard pond, from liners and pumps to aquatic plants—even baby fish.

Seeds of Change (888–762–7333, www.seedsofchange.com)

Anything you buy from this site—seeds, seedlings, fruit trees, produce—is certified organic. Check out the seed collections for children's gardens, fall color, patio gardening in pots, and even for inexperienced gardeners.

Southern Exposure Seed Exchange (540–894–9480, www.southernexposure.com)

This company specializes in heirloom varieties and open-pollinated seeds—which haven't been hybridized for modern preferences of color, bloom times, and other factors. In other words, they're antique flowers and vegetables, and many people swear that they're better than today's varieties.

Van Dyck's (800–248–2852, www.vandycks.com)

A source for top-quality bulbs and perennials at wholesale prices.

NEED MORE GARDENING INFO?

Head to the local library and look up the latest edition of the National Garden Book *(Sunset), which offers excellent information about a host of garden plants and how-to instructions for many common gardening procedures, such as rooting cuttings, pruning shrubs, and starting from seeds. If your library doesn't have it, ask to get it, or pick up your own paperback copy.*

TIME IS MONEY—SO PLANT A CARE-FREE GARDEN

Most gardens need a lot of watering, weeding, and pruning, but yours doesn't have to, if you:

- Think about plants' ultimate sizes. That new tree, plant, shrub, or perennial looks small now, but you may someday find yourself having to prune it all the time to keep it from getting too big for its location. So always check the label or catalog description to see what the plant's ultimate size will be, and don't buy something that's going to get too big for the spot. Choose a smaller plant—or even a dwarf variety—and save yourself a whole lot of pruning later.

- Don't plant things too close together. It's hard to do when the plants are small, but always follow the spacing guidelines provided by the nursery. Those baby plants might look a bit sparse at first, but you'll save yourself having to transplant them later when they start growing together (unless you're trying to create a hedge, in which case you'll want to squeeze the spacing).

- Simplify watering. There's an inexpensive product that makes watering easy, ensures that no water gets wasted—and makes for healthier plants, too. It's called a drip hose and it has holes along its length that let out a steady trickle of water. Snake a drip hose between a group of plantings and all you need to do is turn on the spigot when it's time to water. (Connect it to a simple mechanical timer at the spigot and you won't even have to do that.) You'll be delivering the water right to the roots, which is efficient because it reduces evaporation and healthy because it prevents diseases that can occur when foliage is frequently wet.

- Mulch. Many homeowners think of mulch as little more than a tool for beautifying their yards, but it's actually a time and money saver as well. A good bed of chopped wood, bark, or leaves helps keep the soil moist, reducing the watering requirements of the garden. It also blocks many weed seeds from sprouting, and it gradually feeds the plants organic nutrients as it decomposes. Make your own mulch by putting your fall leaves through a shredder, which you can buy at www.gardeners.com. Then cover your garden beds—and drip hose—with it.

GOOD DEALS MAKE GOOD NEIGHBORS

Here's a great way to save money on big, expensive outdoor tools that you don't use very often, such as snowblowers and 36-foot extension ladders: Share them with a few neighbors. Split the cost equally, and store the goodies at the house where they'll be easiest for everyone to access. Just make sure to come to an agreement—preferably in writing—about what you'll do if one of the participants moves off the block. The easiest solution is that the other neighbors simply reimburse him for his initial investment, if he even bothers to ask for his money back, so make sure to record the numbers or save the purchase receipt. (A good way to pay for service on shared gas-powered equipment is to invite an additional neighbor to buy into the deal for the cost of a tune-up.) Sharing the cost of tool rentals—power washers, lawn aerators, and so forth—is simpler to arrange since you need only split the onetime cost of the rental itself.

Go Native

Your yard will need a lot less maintenance, fertilizer, and watering if you plant native species. After all, native trees, shrubs, and ground covers feel perfectly at home in your climate, so they'll grow almost like weeds. If you live in an arid region, go with a succulent garden. If you live in a woodland, create a canopy of trees. If you live in the prairie, create a wildflower meadow. And wherever you live, minimize your lawn, since turfgrass isn't the natural state of things anywhere. You can convert labor-intensive grass to other plantings that grow without the need for mowing, weeding, and reseeding. There are many alternatives, from flowering ground covers to ornamental grasses.

MAXIMIZING SMALL YARDS

To get the biggest impact from a modest planting space—or from any yard—think about creating a garden that will be interesting in all four seasons. It's easy. Any good nursery or garden catalog will offer everything you need, such as a mix of bulbs that bloom through spring, flowering shrubs that stagger their blooms through summer, plants with colorful fall foliage and berries, and ornamental grasses that hold their seedpods all winter.

DON'T WASTE YOUR MONEY ON

■ DON'T WASTE YOUR MONEY ON

. . . A LEAF BLOWER.

Unless you spend a few hundred dollars, you're going to wind up with a blower that barely has the power to extinguish birthday candles, never mind moving vast piles of leaves, acorns, and twigs across your lawn. So save yourself some money—as well as the frustration of mixing gas and oil or managing long power cords—and buy a good old-fashioned leaf rake.

CHEAP FENCES

When the neighbors are too close for comfort, there's no better investment than a big privacy fence to make them feel a little farther away. Fences aren't cheap, but there are two good ways to save:

1. Plant a living fence. They won't do the job as quickly as a wood or plastic fence, but given enough time to become a thick hedge, plants can provide just as much screening and security. And if you start with small specimens, your fence will cost a tiny fraction of even the cheapest home center pickets. Just make sure to choose evergreen plants so you'll get year-round coverage, and if you want to keep pets and people out, look for something with thick foliage (or even for the razor-sharp leaves of certain hollies).

2. Share the cost. Whether you're going with a living fence or one built from wood or vinyl, it's a good idea to talk with the neighbors on the other side before the fence goes in. It's a chance to put a friendly spin on things, make sure everyone is in agreement about property lines—and ask them to split the cost with you. After all, they'll get the benefits, too

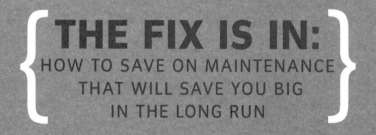

THE FIX IS IN:
HOW TO SAVE ON MAINTENANCE
THAT WILL SAVE YOU BIG
IN THE LONG RUN

Use it up, wear it out, make do,
or do without.

—Yankee proverb

This is where many homeowners go wrong: Pinched by the high cost of room and board, they skimp on the routine maintenance of their homes, from annual service for the furnace, to repairing a faucet that starts to drip, to touching up spots where the exterior paint is peeling. But ignoring problems like these actually doesn't save money—in fact, it can be extremely pricey, because it may cost much more to fix problems later than to nip them in the bud now. That oil burner is going to burn more oil if it's not tuned up, for example, and lack of maintenance could even cause it to break down and require costly repairs. Not only will the steady drip of a faucet increase your water bill, but what began as a simple fix can easily grow into a rusted-out faucet that needs total replacement. Peeling paint is going to worsen quickly if it isn't repaired—it could even lead to rotting of the siding. And pretty much any other skipped maintenance can have equally costly results. So just because you're strapped for cash doesn't mean you should strap on the blinders and ignore the problems that inevitably occur in every house. Here's a guide to keeping everything running right—*without* breaking your bank account.

CHECK IT TWICE: SEASONAL MAINTENANCE CHECKLISTS

To resolve small problems before they become large ones and large ones before they cause collateral damage, you'll need to watch, sniff, and listen for signs of trouble. The following checklists should help you keep the house humming and money in your pocket.

Each Spring

☐ Clean out the gutters. This prevents built-up debris from causing dams that can send water rushing into your home. You'll want to scoop out leaves and other debris, check all the joints, reattach any loose fasteners, and flush out any clogs in the downspouts with a garden hose and forceful spray attachment.

☐ If you have central air-conditioning with a media filter, change the filter before the cooling season begins.

☐ Press the test buttons on each of your smoke and carbon monoxide detectors (which belong in every bedroom and hallway, as well as in the basement and garage). You should replace your detectors every five to ten years. The International Association of Fire Chiefs recommends changing the batteries when you move the clocks ahead for daylight saving time, but you don't necessarily have to do that as long as you have detectors designed to chirp when the batteries get low. (Of course, somehow these batteries always manage to go dead in the middle of the night, waking everyone up and causing a drowsy search for the beeping detector.)

☐ Check the pressure valves on your fire extinguishers to make sure they're still charged.

☐ Cut back overgrown foundation plantings to ensure that there's at least a foot of airspace between the vegetation and your building.

☐ If you have "triple-track" storm windows, lift the storms and lower the screens. If you have another type of storm windows, exchange them for the screens.

Each Fall

☐ Clean out the gutters again, when you do the final leaf cleanup of the season. Scoop out leaves and other debris, check all the joints, reattach any loose fasteners, and flush out any downspout clogs with a garden hose.

☐ If you have an oil-burning furnace and/or water heater, hire your oil company to come clean the burner and service the system before the heating season begins.

☐ If you have hot-water heat, bleed the air out of the system the first time you run it for the season by opening the valves on the radiators until the first drips of water come out.

☐ If you have forced-air heat with a media filter, change the filter before the heating season begins.

☐ Press the test buttons on your smoke and carbon monoxide detectors (which you should have in every bedroom and hallway, as well as in the basement and garage). Change the batteries unless you have detectors that chirp when the batteries get low.

☐ Check the pressure valves on your fire extinguishers to make sure they're still charged.

☐ Cut back overgrown foundation plantings to ensure that there's at least a foot of airspace between the vegetation and your building.

☐ If you have "triple-track" storm windows, lift the screens and lower the storms. If you have another type of system, exchange the screens for the storms.

At Least Monthly (for seasonal items, only when in use)

☐ If you have forced-air heat or a central air-conditioning unit with a prefilter on the intake vent, change it monthly.

☐ If you have steam heat, check the water level every month during the heating season. Also, flush out the sediment that collects in the overflow valve.

☐ Watch for signs of water on ceilings, around skylights, in sink cabinets, under bathrooms, around windows, and in the basement and attic. If you find a roof or gutter leak, call in a roofer immediately. If you find a plumbing problem, call a plumber immediately.

☐ Stay alert for musty smells in the basement and the vanities and cabinets under sinks. These odors are surefire indications that there's a moisture problem to be addressed (see "What You Need to Know About Mold" in this chapter).

☐ Listen for toilets that run. This happens when the valve isn't closing properly as the tank refills; it just keeps on filling and leaking into the bowl. That's a major waste of water. If you're unsure whether a toilet is running, put a few drops of food coloring into the tank, then let the toilet sit for an hour or so without flushing. If you see the color bleed into the bowl, you have a running toilet. You can buy repair kits for this problem, but every toilet is different, so you may be better off hiring a plumber. (Avoid replacing your toilet if it was installed before 1991, because toilets made after that date generally don't work as well as ones made before it, thanks to an environmental law that limits how much water they consume with each flush.)

☐ Before the first frost, disconnect your garden hose and close the shutoff valve for the exterior faucet from inside the home. Otherwise water in the pipes can freeze, expand, and possibly crack the hose, the faucet, or even the supply pipe, which can cause a major leak.

Every One to Three Years

☐ Remove the exhaust duct from the back of the clothes dryer and vacuum the machine's outlet to eliminate lint buildup. Vacuum out the duct as well, or simply replace it with a new one. (Make sure to use only metal pipe, either rigid or accordion style.)

☐ If you have a recirculating range hood (versus one that exhausts to the outside), replace the air filter. Whatever kind of hood you have, wash the grease filters as well. (You may need to take both these steps more often if you do a lot of frying.)

☐ Check the basement walls for cracks, which you can seal with concrete caulk, or holes, which you can patch with hydraulic cement. For porous concrete walls, paint with Drylok Masonry Treatment. If the air is excessively humid, consider getting a dehumidifier.

☐ Check the attic for dampness on the underside of the roof. If you find any, contact a roofer.

☐ Check the pipe connections around your garbage disposal and tighten them by hand if they've loosened up from the machine's vibration.

☐ Hire a professional chimney sweep to inspect and clean your chimney flues.

☐ Check the caulk seal around the perimeter of your bathtub. If it's cracked or blackened, remove it by cutting it free with a sharp utility knife. When the surface is totally dry, replace it with high-quality bathroom caulk.

☐ Vacuum the dust from your refrigerator's condenser. On older models, the grill is on the back of the fridge. On newer ones, it's on the bottom—to access bottom coils, remove the front toe kick, and use a narrow-tipped vacuum head to clean underneath.

☐ Hire an air-conditioning service company to tune up your central air system.

☐ Lubricate your garage door wheels with a spray product sold for that purpose.

☐ Watch for peeling exterior paint and touch up problem areas by scraping loose spots, priming with an oil-base primer, and then repainting with leftovers from the last time the house was painted. This will help delay the eventual complete repainting that every wood-sided house needs.

☐ Remove the registers or grilles from heating and air-conditioning outlets, vacuum them, and vacuum as far into the ducts as you can reach with your household vacuum. This reduces the dust in the ducts, which can otherwise breed mold.

☐ Exercise your electrical circuit breakers by switching each one to the off position and then back on again. This prevents corrosion between the contacts, which could otherwise hinder the breaker from tripping in the event of an electrical overload.

☐ Test the ground fault circuit interrupter outlets in your kitchen, bathrooms, basement, garage, and outdoors by pressing the TEST button and checking that the power has indeed been disabled. Then press the RESET button to restore power. (Ground fault outlets protect against electrocution, and should be installed wherever there's a water source nearby. If you don't have them in your kitchen, bathrooms, basement, garage, or exterior outlets, hire an electrician to install them—or do it yourself if you're experienced with electrical wiring.)

☐ If you have a septic system or a well, have it checked by a licensed well or septic service contractor and serviced as necessary.

WHAT YOU NEED TO KNOW ABOUT MOLD

A few years back, the mold rush was on. There were highly publicized cases of "toxic mold" causing everything from blurred vision to headaches, nausea, and memory loss in adults. There were million-dollar court awards against homebuilders and insurers, and numerous school buildings were razed entirely. Homeowners were being told that any mold in their houses—and there's some mold in the vast majority of houses—had to be removed immediately, by men in contamination suits.

So why don't you don't hear much about mold anymore? The biggest reason is that the insurance industry has rewritten its policies to severely limit mold coverage. That dried up the lawsuits and much of the funding for remediation. Meanwhile, medical researchers have also had a hard time proving that toxic molds can actually release airborne toxins in high enough levels to have any effect whatsoever on human beings. That's still an open—and hotly debated—question.

The vast majority of household mold isn't the toxic kind anyway, though it can still cause allergies and asthma. Ever have a sneezing attack when you headed down into the basement to do laundry? Even if you're not allergic to mold, the odors can be embarrassingly unpleasant. And some molds can also cause the wood structure of your house to disintegrate (what's known as dry rot).

Luckily, preventing mold and even removing small colonies that do form are easy and inexpensive do-it-yourself jobs.

Preventing Mold

Mold spores are in the air all around us, and will grow colonies of mold wherever any material with organic content—wood, wallboard, soap scum, wallpaper, dust, paint, paper, fabric, and more—gets and stays damp. It takes only twenty-four to seventy-two hours for mold to form, so it's essential that you dry up any water problems immediately. Hire a plumber to fix leaking pipes, a roofer to resolve gutter or roofing problems, and a basement waterproofing company to seal a wet basement. Also, make sure that your clothes dryer is vented outside, always use your bathroom vent fan during and for twenty minutes after showers, and install a dehumidifier if your basement is excessively humid.

Removing Mold

If you find a small patch of mold in your home, you can generally kill it yourself. For starters, dry up the moisture source that's feeding the mold. Then get everyone else out of the house and open the windows. Don an N-95 respirator, rubber gloves that extend up your forearms, and safety goggles (without ventilation holes). Scrub mold off nonporous surfaces such as ceramic tiles and bathroom fixtures using a detergent that contains bleach, such as Tilex, or a 10 percent solution of bleach in water. Replaceable porous surfaces like wallboard, insulation, acoustical tile, and carpets should be cut out and thrown away. If wood framing is infested, soak it with the bleach solution to kill the mold.

THE CATCH People with mold allergies, asthma, or weakened immune systems should not attempt to do their own mold remediation.

You can download an Environmental Protection Agency booklet about dealing with mold at www.epa.gov/mold/images/moldguide.pdf.

COOL BY NATURE

If you don't have air-conditioning, the following tricks will make the summertime a lot more comfortable. If you do, they will slash your electricity bills:

- Plant a tree. Putting a large shade tree on the southern exposure of your house can help cool it in summer months by reducing the amount of solar heat absorbed through the windows, the siding, and especially the roof.

- Open windows from above. Most people open double-hung sash windows— that is, the standard type of window with two panes that slide up and down—by lifting the lower sash. But since heat rises, you'll flush out more hot air by lowering the upper sash (assuming they're not painted shut).

- Open attic windows in summer. If you have windows on the gable ends of your unfinished attic, opening them slightly during the hot months of the year will help ventilate heat that gets trapped up there, effectively cooling the whole house. If you have an attic fan, adjust the thermostat so it's running on hot days.

- Use "sunblock": Close curtains and shades on hot days to block out solar heat. Conversely, make sure to open shades and drapes on sunny days in the winter to allow passive solar energy to enter the house. In either season, it's the south-facing windows that matter most.

- As often as possible, turn off unneeded light fixtures and lamps during the daylight hours. The bulbs create heat. Also, make sure to turn off your heating system during the off season. Otherwise boilers will keep their tanks of water hot, and furnace pilot lights will give off unwanted heat.

- Install ceiling fans. Okay, these aren't free and they don't exactly qualify as natural, but they are a very inexpensive and effective way to cool your house—and will make sleeping a lot more comfortable if installed directly over your bed. Set your ceiling fans to spin counterclockwise in summer, because this blows air onto your skin, creating a windchill effect. (Then switch to a clockwise rotation, and run them on low, for winter in order to create a slight updraft that forces the warm air trapped at the ceiling back down into the living space.)

A BASIC TOOL KIT

There's nothing quite so frustrating as realizing you don't have the right tool for the job—especially if you've just spent a lot of energy diagnosing a problem, planning your repair, and buying other supplies and tools that you knew you'd need. On the other hand, who can afford the thousands of dollars in professional-quality tools that every television how-to guru seems to have at his disposal? Well, not to worry. Here's a rundown of a basic tool collection every home should have. (You can create an electronic wish list that friends and relatives can see at Amazon.com or WishList.com, or just try leaving a handwritten list around where friends can see it just before your housewarming party or birthday.)

THE CATCH You'll find yourself needing other tools that aren't on this list, but at least these will give you a good start.

For the Kitchen

- 6-in-1 screwdriver. These handy tools can quickly convert between two sizes of Phillips and two sizes of flathead screwdriver. That's only 4-in-1, of course; the manufacturers like to tout the two extra screwdriver tubes as nut drivers, but you'll probably never use them since there are only two sizes.

- Fire extinguisher. Hang it in a closet or stash it under the sink, and make a mental note of where it is. Also, check its charge now and then, and replace as necessary. (You should also have an extinguisher near your bedrooms and another one near the heating plant.)

- Maglite Flashlight. These heavy-duty gadgets throw off a bright stream of light—and they're so sturdy, they'll make you feel a little safer walking into the dark basement to check the circuit breaker panel when the power goes out.

For the Toolbox

First of all, you'll want the toolbox itself. A large-capacity plastic box makes a good choice because it's lightweight.

- Hammer. Go for a claw model: The rounded hook is handy for prying up unwanted nails.

- Nail set. This simple item allows you to sink the head of a nail below the surface without denting the wood with your hammer.

- Utility knife. This retractable razor knife is useful for cutting everything from drywall to carpet to rope. (Stock up on plenty of replacement razors too.)

- Tape measure. Here's a case where you'll want to go for the best: a 25-foot-long, 1-inch-wide steel tape, which is big enough for nearly any household job and sturdy enough that it won't fold, even when fully extended.

- Crescent wrench set. It's nice to have a full ratchet set, as well as a whole host of plumbing wrenches, but crescents are an inexpensive and easy starter tool that will get most simple jobs done.

- Needle-nose pliers. There are many different kinds of pliers, but these are great for grabbing small items like wires and headless nails.

- Locking Pliers. These tools grip tightly onto the object they're holding, making them essential for all kinds of tasks.

- Screwdriver set. A good set should have at least three different sizes each of flat- and Phillips-head screwdrivers. Also, look for rubber handles, which are safer for use around electrical wiring.

- Circuit tester. This inexpensive item will confirm that electrical wiring has been shut off before you begin to work on a switch, outlet, or fixture. Get two, and always test wiring using both just to ensure that one tool's bulb hasn't burned out.

■ ONE YOU NEED

HOME REPAIR MANUAL

Be sure to outfit yourself with a copy of the Reader's Digest Complete Do-It-Yourself Manual *(Family Handyman, 2005). The detailed photographs, illustrations, and step-by-step instructions in this hefty book will show you how to do everything from repairing a leaky gutter to refinishing a wood floor.*

- Torpedo level. These little levels are great for checking the position of small shelves, cabinets, and other items that you're hanging.

- Paintbrush. If you're getting only one brush, a 2½-incher is a good choice. Get nylon-and-polyester bristles, because they work with both oil and latex paints.

- Putty knife. This small tool isn't used for cutting, but it does offer invaluable help with scraping and spackling.

- Caulk gun. You'll need one of these to apply caulk around a tub, around a window, or in the cracks in your concrete foundation.

- Cordless drill/driver. You can certainly get away without one of these cordless power tools, which are used for drilling holes and sinking screws. But it's the first power tool any household should own.

Supplies

It's also a great idea to load up on a few basic starter supplies:

- Drywall screws. These are terrific fasteners for a host of different household projects. Buy a one-pound box of each of the following sizes: 3 inch, 1½ inch, and 1 inch.

- Common nails. Again, get a few one-pound boxes in a range of sizes, such as 3 inch, 2 inch, and 1 inch.

- Finish nails. Used on jobs where you don't want the nail heads to be visible, these are essential supplies to keep around the house, in 3 inch, 2 inch, and 1 inch sizes.

- OOK picture hooks. These hardened steel hooks will penetrate even plaster walls without bending or making a large hole. They're rated for hanging pictures of different weights—there are even OOKs designed for concrete apartment walls.

WORTH THE MONEY

ELECTRONIC STUD FINDER

Many household projects, such as repairing trim or hanging shelves, require attaching nails or screws into wall studs for proper support. But first you have to find the studs, and that can be like looking for a needle in a haystack—with the added frustration of poking trial-and-error holes in the wall as you conduct your search. There is an easier way: an electronic stud finder. These devices, which you can pick up at a hardware store starting at less than $20, work something like sonar, except they use electricity instead of sound waves to locate their quarry. They do this by sending low-level electrical charges through the wall and measuring the power of the charges when they return. When the unit crosses a stud, its indicator light comes on, and you know you've hit pay dirt.

THE CATCH

Electronic stud finders don't work well on plaster walls (which are common in houses built before World War II).

FINDING TOOL BARGAINS

You can't beat the prices in the tool corrals, hardware departments, and big box stores such as Home Depot, Lowe's, Sears, and Wal-Mart. These stores also make returns very simple if you order too many 2-by-4s or the wrong kind of tool and want to bring the unused items back. Still, you'll often get a better selection—and certainly better expert advice—at an old-fashioned hardware store, if you're lucky enough to have one in your area (most of them have been forced out of business by the big boxes). You can sometimes find better selection and better prices on tools at the following Web sites as well:

Amazon.com

This all-everything e-tailer has a huge selection in its tools and hardware department, including power, hand, and garden tools—very often with free shipping for small items. But not all of the offerings are small: You can have a gas grill or even a riding mower shipped directly to your door—though you'll pay the freight for oversize items. Amazon has also partnered with numerous independent tool catalogs, so if you order from places like www.toolcrib.com or www.powertools center.net, your order will actually be fulfilled by Amazon anyway.

Aubuchon Hardware (www.hardwarestore.com)

There are 140 Aubuchon hardware stores located throughout New England and New York State, and the century-old company also operates a large mail-order operation. You can order almost everything sold in the stores—from power and hand tools to plumbing and electrical supplies, often with free shipping.

Tool King (www.toolking.com)

This Denver, Colorado, retailer has grown into a huge Internet presence, selling power tools, hand tools, and automotive tools nationwide. The prices and customer service are good, and there's a $7.99 flat shipping rate on most items.

Woodworkers Supply (www.woodworker.com)

This is the place to go for a thorough selection of hard-to-find parts and specialty tools for a wide range of projects. You can get replacement cam locks for assemble-it-yourself furniture that's coming apart at the seams; a wide range of woodworking clamps; sharpening tools for putting an edge back on your knives; and a whole lot of other things that you just won't see on home center shelves.

TORN SCREENS AND BROKEN GLASS

If your new house is an old house, there's a good chance you'll find some cracked glass and torn screens here and there. You can fix these yourself by picking up a screen repair kit at the hardware store and following the enclosed directions, or getting a pane of replacement glass cut to size at a glass shop and following the directions for installing it that you can find in any good home repair manual. But there are downsides: Screen patches can be eyesores, and working with glass is a bit dangerous. Here's a better solution: Bring both problem screens and broken glass to a glass shop for replacement (for $10 to $25 per window). Some glass companies will even come to you and do the repair without so much as removing the window sash.

FREE HOW-TO-DO-IT ADVICE

Even the most left-brained people can't get very far with DIY home repair projects unless they have some thorough and accurate instructions to follow. And those are harder to come by than you might think given the abundance of television shows and publications dedicated to the topic—which are often far too cursory to be of any real help, or are just plain inaccurate in the steps that they recommend. Still, there are some reliable and thorough information sources out there.

This Old House (**www.thisoldhouse.com**)

Unlike many of its imitators, this venerable television show gets all its information straight from a team of professional contractors who were chosen not for their celebrity good looks, but for their status as the absolute best tradesmen in the Boston area, where the show happens to be produced. So the information is always accurate and state of the art. The same crew is behind the information in the show's companion magazine and Web site, which offers a database of previous magazine articles to subscribers.

Fine Homebuilding (**www.taunton.com/finehomebuilding**)

This magazine is aimed at professional builders, but its thorough how-tos are just what amateurs need. And although the projects tend toward high-level work, the instructions are far clearer than what you'll find in publications aimed at an amateur audience. Some simple projects are included, too. You can search the database of all previous issues on the Web site and purchase what you need for a nominal fee.

DON'T WASTE YOUR MONEY ON

. . . A NEW APPLIANCE.

just because your oven is missing a knob or you broke the rotating tray in your microwave. You can order just about any part for any appliance by calling (800) 378–5830. This service, which is a division of Home Depot, will get you what you need—by overnight shipping if you prefer.

DON'T WASTE YOUR MONEY ON

The Local Hardware Store

The guys behind the counter at your local hardware store (if you're lucky enough to have one) aren't usually professional plumbers or carpenters, but they've heard just about every FAQ from homeowners like you. They know what products to use for what job, and you can be sure that they've heard back from their customers about what works—or at least what doesn't. Go into the shop at a quiet moment, pick an employee who looks like he (or she) is old enough to be experienced yet young enough to know about the latest products and trends, flash your best smile, and ask away.

The Home Center

You can also find knowledgeable guys working at the home center—some of them *are* actually professional tradesmen—but the ratio of helpful, experienced workers to surly uninformed staffers at many big box stores is about 1:24. The secret to finding them is to go into the store between nine and five on a weekday. They usually have enough seniority to choose their shifts—and prefer not to deal with the weekend crowds. (Can you blame them?) You can also try going to the customer service desk and asking who really knows about plumbing, plants, or whatever subject you need help with, and then asking the customer service rep to page that person for you.

Your Real Estate Agent

She's not going to teach you how to stop a toilet from running, but the chances are that she knows a good plumber in the area—one who's actually going to show up for a small job, especially if you drop her name. So for those jobs that aren't DIY (do it yourself), let your agent help you HIO (hire it out).

REPAIR OR REPLACE?

What do you do when your DVD player dies? Maybe the problem is minor and easy to fix, but finding qualified repair people certainly won't be simple, and getting the product back and forth to them can mean costly shipping and insurance charges. So as wasteful as it may seem, the better option for many products that break is to simply replace them. As a general rule of thumb, it probably isn't worth trying to repair any electronic device that's more than three years old or that cost less than $200.

EXTENDED WARRANTIES—WORTH THE PRICE?

In a word, no. Electronics retailers love to sell extended warranties and service contracts because they're almost pure profit for the stores. The vast majority of people forget about the coverage almost as soon as they leave the store, so only a tiny fraction of customers ever utilize the free maintenance that is sometimes included with the service plans. And chances are small that you'll ever need to collect on the warranty, either. You're better off putting all the money you could have spent on an extended warranty or service contract into a contingency fund in case of problems.

For the most part, the same goes for warranties related to the home itself, such as water-line insurance and whole-home warranties. There are certainly people who have had major disasters and have been bailed out by their extended warranties, but for every one of these folks, there are thousands who've never had a problem that was covered by their plans.

There is one exception to this rule, however: oil-company service contracts, which generally come with one free annual service for your oil burner, something you definitely need. These plans cost only slightly more than what you'd pay for the tune-up alone, and they also provide you with free twenty-four-hour emergency service. That's money well spent for an oil-burning system, especially if it's aging.

PREVENTING TERMITES AND CARPENTER ANTS

To you, it's a house. To termites, it's an all-you-can-eat buffet. These pests live in the soil in every state except Alaska, and they send out flying swarms in search of wood to eat. If they discover your house, they'll quickly establish a new colony—about one million strong—in the ground nearby and set about devouring the framing, flooring, siding, and other wood parts. It takes many years, but in extreme cases they can eat so much structural wood that buildings collapse. So if you see flocks of winged insects inside your home in spring, or pencil-wide mud tubes across surfaces in your basement, you've likely got an infestation, and you should call in a professional pest control company to investigate. For a searchable database of recognized companies, go to www.pestworld.com.

Extermination can be costly, but termite prevention is actually fairly simple and inexpensive. There are three keys to keeping termites (and other wood-damaging insects, such as carpenter ants) out of your home:

1. Stay dry. Bugs like damp wood, so the best way to keep them out is to keep the water out. Have leaking roofs, gutters, and plumbing fixed immediately—and grade your yard away from your house's foundation.

2. Guard the perimeter. Cut bushes back so they're at least a foot away from the house. Rake mulch as far as possible from siding—18 inches is ideal. And move firewood at least 15 feet from the house.

3. Go nontoxic. Borax, a detergent sold at hardware stores, is no more harmful to humans than table salt (in fact, it's used as a food additive in some countries), but it's a powerful insecticide. So sprinkle the powder in any pest-prone area. (Just make sure to use it only in places that don't get wet, since it's water soluble.) For more information, go to www.doityourself termitecontrol.com.

BOOST YOUR CURB APPEAL

First impressions are everything, whether you're hosting a dinner party, having your future in-laws for a visit, trying to get your new neighbors to like you, or selling your home. And when it comes to houses, making a good first impression means giving your house curb appeal. You can't make a boxy 1970s ranch look like a grand Victorian mansion, of course, but you can show any house at its best, and it won't cost you much dough:

- Clean up. Be meticulous about picking up twigs that fall from trees, litter that collects on the grass, and leaves that drop in autumn. And always keep your walk, sidewalk, and driveway well swept.

- Touch up. Scrape away any paint that's peeling on the front of the house, then apply primer and some of the paint left over from the original paint job, if you have it.

- Dress up. Give your house some sort of appealing quirkiness. You might hang your street numbers in an unusual spot, paint the front door in a bold and surprising color, or hang flower boxes from the windows.

- Flower up. Try to choose an array of plantings that will bloom at different times so you have something colorful in your front yard throughout the growing season, from spring flowers to fall foliage.

{ **GETTING AN UPGRADE:** THE D-I-WHYS, WHY-NOTS, AND WHEREFORES OF HOME IMPROVEMENTS }

How large an income is thrift.

−Marcus Tullius Cicero

This is today's version of the American dream: Get a great deal on a home that's got potential but needs some TLC, and then roll up your sleeves and transform it from funky to fantastic. For some people the dream continues with immediately selling the house for a big profit and starting all over again with a bigger one. Others are content to take their time with the improvements and to live for a while in the place they've worked so hard to create. Whichever way you lean, there's good news: Home improving—from applying fresh paint and wallpaper, to opening up the floor plan, to upgrading old fixtures—isn't only the province of the super-rich or super-handy. You just need to stage the work in affordable chunks, contribute plenty of your own sweat equity to the projects, and understand a few simple tricks for getting the most bang for your renovation buck.

TO DIY OR HIO, THAT IS THE QUESTION

Whether you're painting the house, replacing your bathroom faucet, laying a new tile floor, or doing any number of other home improvement projects, doing it yourself (DIY) can save you big bucks over hiring it out (HIO). A job that you'd pay a contractor $10,000 to do, for example, might cost you only $1,000 in materials (even when you include the cost of a how-to book and late-night Chinese takeout for your volunteer crew when the job is done).

But doing it yourself isn't always the best idea. It can take many months to complete a big job if you're working only on weekends and holidays. You can make amateur mistakes that mean the job doesn't look right, or even that you need to hire a professional to fix it in the end anyway. And of course, you can hurt yourself or cause a safety hazard in your home. So here are three questions that will help you assess the merits of DIY or HIO for any home improvement job:

1. *What's the risk?* Think twice, obviously, before tackling projects that involve danger, such as anything that puts you on the top of a 36-foot ladder, involves heavy-duty cutting equipment like a chain saw, or requires complicated electrical wiring that could create a fire or electrocution hazard if done improperly. Cosmetic projects such as interior painting, tile work, and finish carpentry, on the other hand, often don't involve much safety risk. Still, their results will be in plain sight for everyone to see for a long time. So they involve a different kind of risk: that your mistakes—from splotchy paint to uneven tiles to hammer-dented woodwork—simply won't look very good.

2. *Do I have the right experience?* A good rule of thumb is to do what you know. If you spent a few summers in college working on a housepainting crew, painting is probably well within your comfort zone. If you once helped a friend wallpaper her bedroom or install a new bathroom vent, these may be projects you can easily handle yourself. Of course, you can always tackle a project you've never done before. Just make sure to pick up a good how-to book; to start the job in an out-of-the-way location, if possible, so you make your rookie mistakes there; and to draft an experienced pal, at least to get you started.

3. ***What's the disruption factor?*** One of the biggest drawbacks of doing a big project yourself is that it's going to take awhile. And that's not just because you don't work as fast as a professional; it's because you'll be doing the work piecemeal on weekends, holidays, and perhaps nights. That's why jobs that take place far away from the comings and goings of day-to-day life in your home—say, finishing an attic, installing a garage organizing system, or updating a spare bathroom—are much better suited to DIY than are jobs that will cause major household interruptions, like any project that involves disabling the kitchen or a primary bathroom for more than an hour or two.

With all of that said, there is often a third option besides DIY or HIO. You can sometimes hire a contractor to do the job, but stipulate in the contract that you'll handle certain aspects of the work yourself in exchange for a discount on the total price. You may be able to do the demolition of your kitchen before it gets rebuilt, for example, or to remove and reinstall the storm windows for a professional house-painting crew. Conversely, if you're handling a large job, such as finishing the attic, yourself, you can always hire pros to take on some of the trickier aspects of the job, like wiring in the electricity or hanging and taping the drywall.

(OR RIDICULOUSLY CHEAP)

■ **GET IT FOR FREE**

DIY CLASSES

A great way to learn how to do something yourself is to attend a clinic at your nearest home center, such as Home Depot or Lowe's. The instructor will demonstrate the procedure for, say, hanging wallpaper or building a pavestone walkway, and you'll get a chance to try your hand at the job. The classes are free, and every home center offers them on a weekly basis.

THE CATCH You won't learn everything you need to know at the clinic, so make sure to get a step-by-step instruction book as well. }

ONE-STOP SHOPPING: BIG BOX INSTALLERS

There is an alternative to the laborious task of searching for a contractor, at least for straightforward installation projects that don't involve multiple trades: Home centers such as Home Depot and Lowe's will install the vast majority of the products that they sell, from bathtubs to patio stones.

You will get the work done quickly and without the stress of the contractor hunt.

THE CATCH The installation crews may not be experienced tradesmen; in some cases they've been trained quickly in the specific process they're being sent to do and can make mistakes if your job presents challenges they haven't seen before.

HIRING RELIABLE TRADESMEN

Half of the reason that we've all become DIYers these days is that it's so difficult to find reliable professionals to do the work. It's hard to get good contractors even to return your phone call, let alone take on your project, especially if it's a small job. Things are so bad that when a contractor actually does show up and express interest in the work, you might find yourself wondering what's wrong with the guy that's making him so desperate.

It wasn't always this way. There was a time when reliable, knowledgeable, trustworthy building professionals were as easy to find as reliable, knowledgeable, trustworthy doctors. But then something happened and the pool of professional tradesmen changed dramatically. That something was the rise of the personal computer and the Internet. Thanks to the (at least perceived) big-money jobs in computers, a lot fewer high schoolers have been choosing the plumber, carpenter, or electrician programs at vocational schools. As a result, there are fewer tradesmen around, and contractors have a hard time filling their crews with quality workers. Meanwhile, the renovation market is booming, so contractors—even lousy ones— have more work than they can possibly handle.

How can you find a good contractor and convince him to do your job? Well, there's no magic bullet, but here's the best approach to take:

1. Put down the phone book. Throw away the advertisements that come in the mail. The way to find your contractor is by word of mouth: Ask neighbors, friends, and acquaintances. Ask the guy at the local hardware store. And ask other building professionals—for example, if you have a plumber whom you like, ask her for a referral for that electrician you need. Keep at it until you get three to six referrals.

2. Call each recommended professional. When you leave a message, remember that you're trying to sell your project to him as much as you are deciding whether he's someone that you want to hire. Drop the name of the person who recommended him. Tell him that you've heard he's great at what he does..

3. Set up appointments with the contractors you hear back from. Don't try to chase down the ones who don't return your messages. If they don't call you back now, they won't call you back during the job, either, and you don't want that.

4. Walk the job with each contractor, explaining in as much detail as possible exactly what you want and listening to her take on the best way to do the job. Then ask her for a written bid and a list of twelve or more references.

5. Call a random selection of references from the list. Ask them what sort of project the contractor did for them, whether they like the results, how she was to work with, and whether they'd hire her again.

6. Compare the bids not solely on price, but on professionalism as well. If you've laid out a specific project, the bid should be itemized with prices for each element of the job. If any contractor's bid is much higher or much lower than the pack, throw it away. He's either lowballing in the hope of winning the job—in which case you can be sure the price will increase later—or he's highballing because he's really too busy, but would rather price himself out than say no.

7. Make your choice based on their original referrals, references, profession-alism, and approaches to your job—and on your gut.

8. Call the winner and tell him you want him to do the job. Drop the name of the referrer again. If he tells you that he's too busy, tell him that you're willing to wait for quality. Ask him when he could get to your project, and if you really can wait, ask him to put you on his calendar for that time slot.

GET HELP FINDING HELP

There's no substitute for getting referrals from your friends and neighbors, but there are a few resources that can make it easier to determine whether building profes-sionals are reliable—before you hire them.

Quality Ratings

A couple of Web sites offer recommendations for building professionals based on reviews from their previous clients:

Angie's List (www.angieslist.com)

More than 350,000 members of this Web site have posted their comments about building professionals in thirty-eight cities across the country. If you're in one of the communities covered by the list, you can join up and check out the reports on tradesmen in your area. You will have to pay about $60 for a yearlong member-ship—member dues are what support the site, which accepts no advertising or placement fees in order to maintain its objectivity.

The Franklin Report (www.franklinreport.com)

If you live in Los Angeles, Chicago, southeastern Florida, or New York City—or the suburbs of Westchester County, New York, and Fairfield County, Connecticut—don't miss this rating service for home professionals, from air-conditioning contractors to window washers and everything in between. The information is based on surveys of the companies' former customers and industry peers. The publisher claims that the most thorough reviews are reserved for its annual book, but you don't need to shell out $22.50 to buy this tome; plenty of information is available for free on the Web site.

Trade Groups

Just because she's a member of a trade group doesn't mean that a contractor is any good, or that you can skip doing a reference check on her, but it does indicate that she's serious enough about her job that she's willing to pay membership dues.

National Association of Home Builders (800-368-5242, www.nahb.org)

The NAHB is a trade group for contractors around the country. You can find a ton of useful articles on its Web site, and you can search for a remodeling contractor in your zip code. You can also find a local branch office of the NAHB and call for more specific advice—including ballpark costs for whatever job you're planning.

National Association of the Remodeling Industry (800-611-6274, www.nari.org)

This trade group is a competitor of the NAHB that focuses only on remodeling as opposed to all types of residential construction. It, too, offers a searchable database of member contractors by zip code.

National Kitchen & Bath Association (800-843-6522, www.nkba.org)

Another trade group with a database of members, this one caters to professionals who will help you plan and outfit your kitchen or bathroom makeover, typically for a nominal fee that's included in the price of the products you purchase.

Referral Services

These free services promise to match you with prescreened contractors in your area, and they can be a good way to find a pro, if you proceed with your eyes wide open. In other words, don't count on the Web site to truly have screened anyone. While it's probably true that a contractor who has been the subject of numerous complaints will stop being recommended, for the most part the site is going to be a willing matchmaker for any contractor willing to pay its listing fee.

- www.reliableremodeler.com
- www.renovationexperts.com
- www.servicemagic.com
- www.1800contractor.com

■ GET IT FOR FREE

GET IT FOR FREE

HOW-TO BOOKS

Need a good guidebook to walk you through a weekend project such as laying a new tile countertop or spackling a pockmarked plaster wall? Hit the library. In many towns you can search the library's book catalog over the Internet. If your local library doesn't carry the book you need, you can request that they get it for you from another library using the interlibrary loan system.

THE CATCH

Books in the reference department cannot be taken home, but you can spend a few dimes to photocopy the relevant pages on the library's copier.

}

THE BARTER SYSTEM

Imagine getting the electrical wiring installed for your new basement rec room without paying for the labor—without paying money, that is. Instead you simply return the favor by providing your own skilled labor for the electrician, perhaps giving her guitar lessons or tutoring her child. This is the barter system, of course, and it's a great way to cut back on your home improvement costs—especially since it means you don't pay sales tax for the work.

The most basic example of bartering for home improvements happens when a couple of friends come to help you paint your house, and then you do the same for them when their houses need the work. But barter doesn't have to be a collaboration of amateurs, and you don't have to provide the same sort of help that you receive. Instead you can trade whatever expertise you have to offer. Does your painter need someone to design him a new Web site? Does your tree trimmer want someone to prepare home-cooked Friday-night meals for her family?

You may not have much luck proposing barter as a form of payment for tradesmen you find through normal channels. It's far easier to establish barter deals with friends and acquaintances in the construction industry. Also, if you run a service business, keep an eye out for clients who are in specific trades and might prefer to pay you with their labor than with cash. Or you can post ads at www.craigslist.org, www.freecycle.org, www.woonba.com, www.tradeaway.com, or www. swapthing.com. Just remember to vet the contractors just as carefully as you would if you were paying them with legal tender.

■ ONE YOU NEED

A SCRAPBOOK

Whether you use a spiral notebook or a true archival scrapbook, it's a good idea to create a journal where you collect information about the improvements, repairs, and changes you make to your house. Whenever you paint, affix the appropriate color cards to a page, with a note about where the colors were used. Stash warranty cards and product information in the scrapbook as well. Always take "before" pictures of any space prior to transforming it, and put these pictures in your journal, too. You'll be glad to have the book later, for both sentimental reasons and practical ones—like matching paint when you do repairs or improvements, and showing potential buyers all the love and care you've given to the house.

ADDING SPACE, ON A BUDGET

Need another bedroom, a family room, or a home office? Building an addition will cost tens or even hundreds of thousands of dollars. Still, there are some ways that you can save money without compromising on quality or using a subpar builder:

- Invest in the bones. Focus your resources on the underlying quality of the project—such as the design, foundation, structural framing, wallboard, and flooring—because these can't be easily upgraded later and, to a large extent, they're what determine the success of the job. If you need to skimp on something, skimp on cosmetic details, such as light fixtures and countertops, which you can easily change out when your budget allows.

- Use existing rooms. Look for ways to add space without the excavation, concrete footings, framing, and roofing that are required when you build an addition. Finishing the basement or attic, for example, or enclosing a screened porch will cost far less than building a new wing off the side of the building. Heck, you may not even need to do much construction at all: If you have an eat-in kitchen, perhaps that rarely used dining room could be appropriated for the home office or spare bedroom you need.

- Stay within the footprint. Even if there's no way around adding new square footage to your home, you may be able to avoid expensive site work. Think about adding *up*—putting a second story onto a one-story home, that is, or a third floor onto a two-story—to avoid the cost of site work.

- Bump out. If a lateral expansion is necessary, you may be able to hang the new space off the side of your building. This kind of addition is called a bump-out, and it requires no earthmoving or foundation work. Of course, you probably can't add 1,000 square feet this way, but you may be able to add 200—enough, perhaps, to accommodate a large soaking tub for your master bathroom or to make room for a breakfast nook in your kitchen.

- Go modular. Another way to save money on a big construction project is to order your addition from a factory. It'll be built to your specifications and delivered fully assembled in modules sized to fit on the back of a truck. And because these factories are located in rural areas with relatively low wages, factory-built additions often cost far less than what people in metro areas would have to pay a local traditional builder. One of the most common modular additions is a "pop-top," where a single family home has the roof removed one day, and a prefab second floor installed and roofed over the next. The new space may be livable in a month or so. See www.havenhomes.com, www.excelhomes.com, and www.modularhousing.com for more information.

BETTER DOORS

One common complaint about first homes is that all the doors are flat plywood "hollow-core" models that look plain—and make the entire house feel plain as a result. Replacing the doors can dress up the whole space, but it's not a DIY job unless you're very experienced with carpentry techniques. Hiring a general contractor to come in and replace the doors with wood-panel versions would cost a small fortune, but there's another solution to consider. Big box home centers such as Home Depot and Lowe's (and if you live out west, a company called Interior Door Replacement Company, 800-366-7776, www.interiordoor.com) will send out crews to measure your doorways and then deliver and install replacement doors. If you choose fiberboard doors that are molded to look just like the wood-panel kind, you may be able to get the job done for as little as $100 per doorway.

HIRING HOUSEPAINTERS

As with finding any tradesmen to work on your house, you'll want to get bids from painters highly recommended by people who've used them, both recently and a few years back (so you can ask how gracefully the work has aged). Here are a few other considerations:

- **Prep school.** Ask all the painters you speak with how exactly they will prep your walls. Expect them to power-wash the house and to remove any failing or overly thick layers of paint. If you're concerned about lead paint, ask them to use dust-capturing sanding equipment or chemical strippers.

- **Keep your roses clean.** The painters should also explain how they'll protect your foundation plantings, decking, patios, driveways, and walks— preferably with plastic tarps that will be laid out each morning and picked up each evening.

- **Ask about the warranty.** Some high-end painters offer written warranties for as long as seven years after the job is complete. Franchises such as

College Pro Painters (www.collegepro.com) and CertaPro Painters (www.certa pro.com) typically offer a two-year written warranty.

- **Brushstrokes.** Make sure that any painters you hire will use paintbrushes to apply the paint. It's okay if they spray or roll the paint onto the walls, but they should "back-brush" the wet paint to work it onto the surface.

DON'T WASTE YOUR MONEY ON

. . . REPLACEMENT WINDOWS OR SIDING.

Replacement windows may improve your home's energy efficiency some-what—but not nearly as much as their marketing flyers claim, because only 20 percent of a home's heat loss happens through the windows anyway. The rest goes through walls, roofs, doors, and gaps in the structure. You can achieve nearly the same efficiency simply by using storm windows and installing foam weatherstripping in the gaps where the upper and lower sash meet, and where the lower sash meets the sill.

If you're considering replacement because your windows don't open and close very easily, or won't stay open without something to prop them up, you just need a little window maintenance. You can hire a contractor or handyman to reconnect the counterweights to the sash, strip away excess paint, and lubricate the jamb with wax—or you can do the job yourself.

Replacement siding, on the other hand, will live up to its promise of eliminating the need to repaint your wood exterior every few years. The problem, though, is that inexpensive vinyl and aluminum products simply don't look as good as real wood. Thus they detract from your curb appeal and, in some cases, the value of your home. And if you have a roof or gutter leak, siding can potentially hide the problem while the walls are rotting underneath it. There are high-quality siding materials that you can use, such as fiber cement, but they cost a small fortune.

THINKING GREEN CAN SAVE YOU SOME GREEN

You can save yourself a lot of money on your addition or renovation project by borrowing some simple green-building techniques:

- Reuse. When you remove trim or paneling, do so carefully and you'll be able to reinstall it later. That'll save you money and ensure that the new installation matches the rest of the space. For trim, gently pry it away from the wall with a flat bar, then use nippers to pull the nails out from the back so you don't mar the good side. For paneling, use a hammer and nail set to drive the nails completely through the paneling so that it comes free.

- Salvage. Before a big old building gets razed to build a new mall, salvage companies usually take out the valuable building materials: not just scrap metal, but also paneling, flooring, plumbing fixtures, chandeliers, fireplace mantels, window sashes, panel doors, and stair railing parts. You can purchase these salvaged materials (see "Salvaged House Parts" in this chapter), or you can reclaim your own. Many homebuilders still don't even try to save the features of homes they're demolishing—all they're thinking about is getting the job done as fast as possible. If you come along at the right moment and offer to strip some materials from the building, they might jump at the chance to reduce the number of Dumpster loads they'll have to cart off the property. Just always ask the project foreman for permission before rummaging around the job site—not only to avoid trespassing, but also for safety's sake.

- Waste not. Another green-building technique that helps the bottom line is the idea of trying to throw away as little as possible from the building site. Scrap lumber and supplies should be stacked and used for small cuts later.

- Be efficient. Green building isn't only about using products that come from environmentally friendly sources; it's also about creating an addition or renovation that's environmentally friendly in its own right. That means creating well-insulated spaces and using high-efficiency equipment to heat and cool them.

Salvaged House Parts

Unless you're searching for something truly one of a kind, it's best to do your salvage shopping locally. Search for "architectural salvage" or "used building materials" at http://local.google.com to find salvage yards near you. Here are some great salvage yards around the country that have online inventories:

Adkins Architectural Antiques & Treasures
Houston, Texas
(713) 522-6547
www.adkinsantiques.com

Architectural Antiquities
Harborside, Maine
(207) 326-4938
www.archantiquities.com

Architectural Emporium
Canonsburg, Pennsylvania
(724) 746-4301
www.architectural-emporium.com

Build It Green!
3-17 Twenty-sixth Avenue (at Fourth Street)
Queens, New York
(718) 777-0132
www.bignyc.org

Materials Unlimited
Ypsilanti, Michigan
(800) 299-9462
www.materialsunlimited.com

Ohmega Salvage
Berkeley, California
(510) 204-0767
www.ohmegasalvage.com

The Old House Parts Company
Kennebunk, Maine
(207) 985-1999
www.oldhouseparts.com

United House Wrecking
Stamford, Connecticut
(203) 348-5371
www.unitedhousewrecking
.com

Will Going Solar Save You Dollars?

Unfortunately, being environmentally friendly doesn't always mean being budget friendly. Installing solar panels on your roof, for example, won't save you any money—at least not yet.

The good news is that today's solar panels look nothing like the giant slabs people installed on their roofs in the 1970s. Now they're hardly even noticeable because they're built right onto the surface of special roofing shingles that get wired together into a hidden solar power generator. And rather than relying solely on their power, you can stay connected to the power grid so you have plenty of juice even on cloudy days. In fact, you can even sell your excess solar power back to the utility company, thanks to special two-way electric meters.

The bad news is that a typical installation costs about $15,000, and your electricity savings simply won't pay back that cost—even if you live in the Sun Belt or in a region with very high electrical prices, and even after you get a tax break from the federal government for a portion of the installation costs.

Still, assuming that the costs of traditional electricity keeps rising, and that solar technology keeps improving, some experts predict that going solar will become a cost-saving alternative over the next decade or so.

NEED A NEW FURNACE?

If the furnace or boiler in your basement is more than a few decades old, chances are that it's extremely inefficient. So replacing it with new, high-efficiency equipment is an upgrade that can literally pay for itself over the next five to ten years thanks to reduced fuel consumption. What's more, many states offer tax rebates to help pay the upfront costs of modernizing—and if you purchase natural-gas-burning equipment, you may qualify for a rebate from the local gas utility as well. To find out about gas rebates, contact your local natural-gas company. For tax breaks on efficiency upgrades, see www.energystar.gov; click on "Special Offers."

ADDITION BY SUBTRACTION

Sometimes the best improvement you can make to your home doesn't involve adding an expensive new product or feature, but simply taking away something that's old and dated:

- Wall-to-wall carpeting. Peel up a corner of the rug to see whether there's hardwood underneath. If there is, removing the old rug is easy. Just don some heavy-duty gloves and pull it up, starting in the corner. Then use a flat bar to remove the "tackless" wood strips from around the perimeter—and watch out for the protruding sharp nails.

  > THE CATCH } The wood floors you uncover will likely need refinishing.

- Linoleum floors. The same holds true for old linoleum floors, if they're worn and dingy. Use a flat bar to pry up the linoleum, which is often multiple layers thick.

  > THE CATCH } Note that some old floor coverings contain asbestos, so hire a pro to remove the built-up layers, or consult a how-to book about taking proper precautions.

- Wallpaper. Still have some stuffy old wallpaper in your home? Replacing it with a nice paint job can instantly brighten and refresh the space. The secret to stripping wallpaper is a cheap tool called a wallpaper scorer, which reduces the amount of elbow grease you'll need for the job because it perforates the paper and allows the stripping solution to get at the glue. You can make your own solution from equal parts warm water and white vinegar. Load it into a plant mister bottle and wet the scored paper thoroughly. Wait fifteen minutes and peel the paper away with a sharp wallpaper scraper. If it doesn't come away easily, spray it again.

- Ugly curtains. It's better to go without window treatments than to live with yellowed old drapes that give your home a haunted-house feeling. If you're good with a sewing machine, you can make your own curtains, or you can buy standard sizes at a home store such as Target, Bed Bath & Beyond, or Linens-n-Things. Or you can order high-quality curtains at reasonable prices from www.countrycurtains.com. You can also remove wood cornices, or you can modernize them with paint and wallpaper decals.

{ INDEX }

{ ABOUT THE AUTHOR }

A former carpenter, Josh Garskof now dons his tool belt only for DIY projects around his own house—or sometimes at friends' homes if he can't come up with a believable excuse fast enough. He writes  about a variety of subjects related to everyday life, including health, money, parenting, and the home. His articles have appeared in *Better Homes and Gardens*, *Parents*, *Popular Science*, *Real Simple*, and the *New York Times*. He is also the author of numerous home improvement books, and is a veteran of the editorial trenches at *Martha Stewart Living*, where he served as executive editor, and *This Old House*, where he was articles editor. He lives with his family in Connecticut.

7/10   (12)   3/10

8/15   (17)   4/15

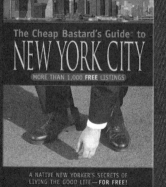

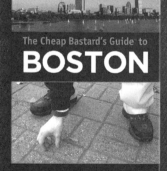